THE SOCIAL SKILLS WORKBOOK FOR KIDS 8-16

150+ PRACTICAL EXERCISES AND ACTIVITIES TO IMPROVE SOCIAL INTELLIGENCE; BUILDING CONFIDENCE, EMPATHY, SELF-ESTEEM, AND COMMUNICATION SKILLS

KILEY HORTON

© **Copyright 2022 - All rights reserved.**

It is not legal to reproduce, duplicate, or transmit any part of this document in either electronic means or in printed format. Recording of this publication is strictly prohibited and any storage of this document is not allowed unless with written permission from the publisher except for the use of brief quotations in a book review.

CONTENTS

Who is Kiley Horton?   9
Introduction   11

1. UNDERSTANDING FEELINGS AND EMOTIONS   17
   What Is Social Intelligence?   17
   What Are Feelings?   21
   What are Emotions?   26
   Your Feelings and Emotions Matter   30
   Know What Makes You Happy   30
   The Emotions of Other People Are also Important   41
   Five Ways to Read Other People's Emotions   43

2. THE BENEFITS OF SOCIALIZING THE RIGHT WAY   47
   Why Is Socializing Important?   47
   Workbook Questions for Self-Reflection about Socialization   54

3. GIVE FIRST: EMPATHY AND COMPASSION   55
   Addressing Your Doubts   56
   Feel What Others Feel   61
   Compassion for Others   64
   Workbook Questions for Compassion and Empathy in Young Children   70

4. WHEN YOU SEEM TO BE RUNNING OUT OF CONFIDENCE   71
   Why Confidence is Important in Socializing   72
   How Do You Know You Lack Confidence?   74

Building Confidence in Yourself Step by Step 75
Workbook Questions for Improving
Confidence for Kids 78

5. NON-VIOLENT COMMUNICATION (NVC) 81
Why Is Communication Skills Development
Important for Children? 81
How Can I Help My Child to Communicate
Effectively? 82
Types of Communication I Need to Know 84
What Is Nonviolent Communication? 85
How Learning Nonviolent Communicate Will
Help Me 87
How to Start and Carry on a Conversation 89
NVC Workbook Questions for Kids 91

6. CONFLICT RESOLUTION: GIVING AND
RECEIVING AND APOLOGY 95
Hating It When You Don't Have Your Way 96
Is Conflict the End of Our Friendship? 100
How to Know if I've Hurt My Friend 102
What to Do If My Friend Hurts Me 104
How to Apologize and Mean It 107
Workbook Questions on Forgiveness for Kids 111

7. MAKING AND KEEPING GREAT FRIENDS 113
What Makes Friendships Important? 114
Who Are Good Friends? 115
How to Make Good Friends 118
Conversation Skills to Nurture Your
Friendship 122

8. PRACTICAL EXERCISES AND ACTIVITIES
GUIDE 125
Activities You Can Do on Your Own 125
Activities to Do with the Help of Your
Parent/Guardian 127
Others: 150+ Practical Exercises And
Activities To Improve Social Intelligence in
Children and Teenagers 129

Conclusion 197
Resources 199

SPECIAL BONUS!

Want this Bonus Book for free?

Get **FREE**, unlimited access to it and all my new books by joining the Fan Base!

SCAN W/ YOUR CAMERA TO JOIN!

WHO IS KILEY HORTON?

Kiley Horton is a mother of two daughters and two sons, as well as an entrepreneur, educator, and author. After experiencing my own issues and having concerns about my first child's learning, development, and behavior, I set out to learn more and discovered that I was extremely passionate about empowering children and adolescents to overcome obstacles and reach their potential.

I understand that working with preteens and teens can be difficult. This is when I decided to help as many children, teachers, parents, and families as she could all over the world.

Since 2004, I've worked as a child development specialist and educational psychology consultant with teachers, parents, and families all over the world.

I teach mindfulness and essential life skills to children, teens, parents, and educators in an engaging, creative, and simplified manner so that they can easily access a sense of contentment, accomplishment, and connection with children and youth.

My proven, effective, and engaging teaching style produces positive results that are sought after on a daily basis.

My primary objectives are to teach children, teachers, and parents how to:

- First, improve yourself so that you can be your best self and role model.
- Have strong communication and social skills, which are essential in all aspects of life;
- Develop emotional intelligence, responsibility, and respect as lifelong problem solvers.
- Teach and parent with empathy, love, logic, and patience.

My husband and I live in Texas with our four children. When I'm not working or spending time with my family, you can find me in the garden, working on an art project in my art studio, or attending a yoga class. Soft-baked cookies and Netflix are two of my weaknesses.

INTRODUCTION

Imagine a young girl walking down the hallway during a break between classes. She isn't chatting with friends or engaging in typical child-like thinking such as, "how many minutes until lunchtime or until I am done with classes for the day?" Instead, she worries about how she looks in her outfit, how her hair is styled, and the complexion of her skin.

She imagines that everyone is looking at her. She thinks that everyone notices her acne, clothes, or that she has put on some weight. For these reasons, she thinks that they are all gossiping about her.

She walks around, feeling like she is living under the spotlight every second of her life.

What's worse, she is scared that her peers will notice her anxiety. For example, they might see her blush when the teacher calls on her in class. Soon, she starts to avoid situations where she is the center of attention. This fear quickly spirals into social anxiety.

The situation has been blown out of proportion ten times over.

And no one understands but you. You've been dealt a great challenge presented to human beings. Being a young adolescent is among the toughest years in a person's life. This is true, and you know it because you are living these years. Your father and mother don't understand; neither do your troublesome little brothers and sisters.

You feel everything more deeply than any of them.

Every day, they keep saying, "You'll get over it." Damn that!

You are living in the moment. What's more, it's a different time we are living in. They may not understand how it feels to live inside themselves. No one is bombarding them with information from one moment to another. They don't have to deal with the bullies at school, and the craziest videos trending on social media.

They don't have to deal with the cool kids, show-offs, the "better-than-yous," the creepy kid at the back of the class who's always making strange noises, and the mean kids who ignore you like you don't exist. Whenever you bump into this group, you find their faithful "worshippers" and "bodyguards" surrounding them.

It's like you can never get a break!

And if you are a guy, it always seems as if others are taller, cooler, and more popular. Your life seems like a trial by your peers.

Life is so unfair.

Why can't you be as confident as Miley Cyrus? If only you could be as popular as Bruno Mars. You know of guys who can walk into a party and have the whole crowd gravitate towards them. They can strike up the right conversations with anyone and keep it going forever. They are friendly, outgoing, and charismatic.

You are not those people and neither are most kids, and that's okay. Social skills and self-confidence don't come naturally to most individuals. Most children have trouble dealing with the emotional turmoil brought by friendship challenges, social expectations, and the compulsion to study.

Such individuals avoid meeting new people and visiting new places. They are scared of small talk because they fear they won't know what to say. Maybe the most difficult part of it all is the unrealistic expectations people put on themselves and the self-loathing that follows.

This anxiety, self-hatred, and hopelessness can lead to emotional and mental breakdowns that hurt the people who love you the most.

As a young adolescent, you are sensitive, and you don't know how to go about attracting and keeping good friends, the ones you can trust with your deepest fears and to help you when you are at your worst.

If you can relate to these struggles, I am so happy you are reading this book.

This book is written to guide you and help you overcome these challenges. You might be pessimistic about the possibilities because you think that's just who you are, but I would appreciate it if you kept an open mind. Reducing social anxiety and improving communication skills, social intelligence, and self-esteem may not come naturally to you, or most of us, but with work, you can improve on them.

My greatest hope is that this book is written in a fun and lively way and that the strategies are also simple and easy to remember.

Regardless of whether you want to stop arguing with your parents, make more friends at school, or be confident around strangers, this book will help you develop the social skills you need to survive in all areas of your life. Some of it may come across as uncomfortable, but that's because life is uncomfortable. You shouldn't miss out on any of these things because they require you to step out of your comfort zone.

Your struggle will be so worth it in the end.

We know that social intelligence is a good life hack to add to your arsenal, so let's get started right away.

I hope you fall in love with this book.

1

UNDERSTANDING FEELINGS AND EMOTIONS

As a workbook that hopes to thoroughly engage young readers, this chapter and the chapters that follow are outlined in simple language with exercises at different points. Chapter one guides the child into the topic of social intelligence without necessarily using jargon. It also aims to help the young reader feel comfortable with the topic and enjoy the first part enough to want to see what else the book holds.

WHAT IS SOCIAL INTELLIGENCE?

The ability to interact and build relationships with empathy and assertiveness is referred to as social intelligence. It arises from self-awareness and effective emotional regulation.

Although it is closely related to emotional intelligence, it is not the same.

Emotional intelligence is derived from self-awareness and includes topics such as emotional awareness and the function of emotions in problem-solving. It has more to do with how people handle themselves before interacting with others.

When you begin interacting with people, social intelligence and emotional intelligence should kick in, covering duties such as expression, discussion, listening, conciliation, and learning through communication with others (Vanessa Van Edwards, 2016).

What are the skills that social intelligence entails?

Social intelligence coordinates the skills needed for effective communication, such as empathy, self-awareness, listening, and emotional reading. These powers are as follows:

1. Fluency in both verbal and nonverbal communication

The most fundamental element of social intelligence is conversational skills. The key venues for transmitting any message are verbal and nonverbal expressions. The first stage of good communication is to use the correct words, the proper tone, and have a clear goal.

2. Understanding of social roles and rules

Knowing a group's social conventions, habits, and quirks is a crucial ability for socially competent people when interacting with them. This makes it easier to interact with people from various social groupings, such as persons of various ages, nationalities, religions, or cultural identities.

3. Ability to listen

The development of social intelligence requires active listening. It facilitates social interaction, reduces conflict, and promotes learning through debate. This has a huge impact on personal development.

4. Being aware of how other people's emotions operate

Understanding what causes people's emotions to be triggered (either adversely or positively) is an important part of practicing empathy. This skill allows for communication that takes into account the characteristics and sensibilities of others, resulting in a message that is both real and successful.

5. Effective social role-playing

This talent enables people to adapt to a variety of social situations. Having a clear understanding of what is expected of us in a range of situations minimizes stress and allows for more constructive relationships.

6. Self-perception and image management

This refers to our capacity to portray ourselves in a way that connects with people while being true to our own selves. The goal is to keep a genuine manner that appeals to others, demonstrates empathy, and promotes our sense of self.

How to Develop Social Intelligence

While some people appear to develop social intelligence without any effort, others must work hard to do so. Fortunately, several tactics can aid in the development of social skills. These strategies can aid in the development of social intelligence:

Pay close attention to what (and who) is around you. People that are socially intelligent are aware of their surroundings and pay attention to subtle social signs. Observe how someone you know interacts with others if you believe they have strong people skills.

Make an effort to improve your emotional intelligence. Emotional intelligence is comparable to social intelligence, but it focuses on how you manage your own emotions and empathize with others. It necessitates identifying when you're having an emotion (which will aid you in recognizing that emotion in others) and effectively managing it. When in a social situation, an emotionally intelligent person can detect and handle unpleasant sentiments such as irritation or wrath

Respect cultural differences. More importantly, look for cultural distinctions to better comprehend them. Although most people develop social skills from their family, friends, and the culture around them, a socially intelligent person recognizes that others' upbringing may influence their responses and habits.

Practice active listening. Work on your communication skills, which necessitate active listening, to improve your social intelligence. Don't interrupt others. Before you answer, take a moment to consider what the other person is saying. Pay attention to the inflections in other people's voices, as they may reveal what they really mean.

Appreciate the people that are significant in your life. People who are socially savvy have strong bonds with those who are important to them. Pay attention to your spouse and children's feelings, as well as the emotions of your friends, coworkers, and other peers. You'll miss out on cues on how to connect with your closest friends if you disregard them.

WHAT ARE FEELINGS?

We frequently experience a range of feelings but cannot articulate what is bothering us or what is happening to us. Actions speak louder than words, demonstrating that we are not our usual selves. The people in our immediate environment are aware of this, but we do not yet know how to respond to it as young adults.

Let us make an effort to comprehend some of the feelings that we experience in our everyday lives and determine whether or not we can find ways to assist ourselves in overcoming them.

What do you have in mind when you say "feelings"?

We refer to feelings as sensations that arise from within or within ourselves. They seldom remain stable for extended periods; rather, they are continually in a state of flux. We experience a wide range of different feelings throughout our lives, including happiness, sadness, worry, and loneliness.

Feelings of Different Kinds

Sadness. Sadness is characterized by feelings of unhappiness and the urge to cry. As a consequence of it, we frequently experience feelings of being drained and fatigued. Even though it is a bothersome sensation, it is natural to have this experience.

When we are depressed, we might not feel like spending time with our friends and would rather be left alone to enjoy some peace.

We are more likely to experience melancholy when we have had a trying day at school, when someone is rude or unkind to us, or when we overhear individuals in our immediate environment arguing.

Long-term depression is not good for your health and should be avoided. When we feel unhappy, it is important to talk to someone and let out how we feel. Never give a second thought to what the opinions of others might be.

You can keep yourself entertained by engaging in an activity that you take pleasure in if you do not wish to inform anyone else. You will immediately be able to tell a change and begin to experience a nicer mood.

Shyness. When you find it difficult to communicate with someone you don't know very well, you may experience the feeling that is known as shyness.

When we experience shyness, the desire to run away or hide from the other person or the situation arises. We may flush or get warm.

When it comes to making new acquaintances, performing in front of an audience, or introducing oneself to a group of people, many people are nervous.

Children who struggle with shyness should try to open up to someone they feel comfortable and care for in their lives. You have no choice but to make an effort to interact with others in the group and strike up conversations with people you already know. It is perfectly normal for children to exhibit hesitant behavior, but as they age, most children outgrow this trait.

You can help timid children or those new to your community or school by being friendly to them, making them feel at ease, chatting with them, and inviting them to play with you.

They will find it much simpler to conquer their shyness with your assistance.

Worrying is something we do when we are concerned that something terrible will happen. Worrying over something can make us physically ill as well as make us feel uneasy. When anxious, our hearts beat faster than normal, and we have problems falling or staying asleep.

When we have not finished an assignment at school or are moving to a new location, we feel anxious about both these situations.

Worrying is bad because it prevents us from thinking clearly. We cease having fun because we're anxious about something.

You may spot a family member or acquaintance who is concerned based on their actions. They might also experience a loss of appetite and high sensitivity to even the smallest annoyances.

Being a good listener is the finest thing you can do to aid someone who is frightened.

Loneliness. This is a prevalent feeling among both young and older adults. When we are lonely, we believe that no one cares about us or wants to spend time with us.

Loneliness makes you want to cry and have sad, bored, and furious feelings.

When you move to a new home or school and are unfamiliar with the other children, you may feel lonely for a few days until you settle in.

Tell an adult whenever you feel lonely. You can ask to go for a stroll or a drive with them. You may enroll in an art or dancing class. A lonely individual is simple to spot because they usually appear unhappy or agitated and sit alone.

You can assist a lonely individual by asking them over to play or by sitting with them and conversing.

How Do I Feel?

Think about how you feel right now.

Now think about how you felt this morning. Do you feel the same way, or do you feel different somehow? Our feelings are always changing because new things are always happening. Highlight all of the feelings that best describe how you've felt today and over the last couple of days.

- Happy
- Excited
- Afraid
- Worried
- Embarrassed
- Confused
- Sad
- Angry
- Shy

- Surprised

Think about each word that you highlighted. Then use each one to complete this sentence:

I felt ---------------------- when --------------------------

----

Did you learn anything? Did any of your answers surprise you?

WHAT ARE EMOTIONS?

Have you ever noticed that some days you have a big smile on your face? You can't wait to hang out with your friends and do all your favorite things. Those days are pretty great, right? You've probably also noticed that some days you don't feel much like smiling at all. You may not want to play with your friends or even eat your favorite food on those days. Those are the days you wish you could skip, right? Whether you are wearing a big smile and laughing or choosing to spend some quiet time alone, you're feeling something. We all experience emotions and feelings every day of our lives—lots of them!

What's the difference between emotions and feelings, anyway? Emotion is how your body behaves when things happen to you. For instance, you may jump in surprise when someone pops out and says, "Boo!" A feeling can follow that emotion. You may feel angry because that "boo" made you spill your drink. Emotions and feelings play a big part in how your day goes. Think about it! Every day is full of new and different things that happen to you. These things give you all kinds of different feelings. Some feelings are good, and some are not so good. It's totally normal for you to have all sorts of emotions and feelings from one day to the next, maybe even from one hour to the next! And guess what? You are not alone. Everyone you know has lots of emotions.

Your feelings can affect how you behave at home with your family, in school with your teachers and classmates, and when you're hanging out with your friends. Emotions and feelings are such a big part of life that it's important to understand them and where they come from. It's really helpful, too. Once you learn what you're feeling and why you will know how to deal with it. You'll also be able to express, or share, those feelings with others in a healthy way, instead of just bottling them up inside you. I promise you, you'll feel a lot better once you do!

Why is it important for youngsters to understand their emotions?

Children need to have an understanding of their feelings for them to be able to deal with them appropriately. Emotional development requires, first and foremost, an awareness of one's feelings and the ability to formulate appropriate responses to one's life experiences.

It can be especially difficult to regulate and keep control of children's feelings and emotions. Through understanding their own and others' feelings and emotions, children will develop the ability to normalize their and others' emotional responses. It might be unsettling to experience a range of feelings without being able to identify them. It is much simpler for children to express their feelings when their emotions are acknowledged and validated. Self-expression has been demonstrated to reduce anxiety, and unresolved feelings can manifest themselves in physical symptoms like migraines. This will enhance their mental as well as their physical health because of these two reasons. So, a happy mind leads to a healthy body!

Furthermore, youngsters have a greater grasp of others' sentiments through comprehending their own emotions. They will be able to empathize with others and strengthen their relationships due to this. This is especially important in the classroom for creating a supportive environment.

The Six Big Emotions

Let's talk about six of the biggest emotions that everyone feels. These emotions can lead you to have lots of different feelings, too.

Happiness: When you feel happy, you might smile or laugh. You might even dance and sing your favorite song. Happiness makes you feel good about things in your life like school, your friends, and that test you aced this morning.

Surprise: You might feel surprised when something happens that you didn't expect. When you feel surprised, you might scrunch up your forehead. This is because you're feeling unsure about what just happened. Your jaw might drop, or you might even jump a little. A surprise can make you feel happy, but it can also make you feel afraid or nervous. It all depends on what the surprise is.

Fear: When you think you're in danger or feel like something bad might happen, you experience fear. If you see a big spider, you might feel afraid. Even giving a report in front of the class can make you feel this way. You may jump back and throw something at the spider, or feel goosebumps or a stomach ache before class.

Sadness: When you feel sad, you might cry or want to be by yourself. This feeling can happen if you lose a pet or even a toy. You might also feel sad from being called names by someone at school or from not making the soccer team.

Anger: If you have ever felt like you were going to explode, you've probably experienced anger. Anger comes when something happens that you don't like. You might feel angry if somebody is being unfair, if you break a favorite toy, or if your mom says you can't sleep over at your friend's house.

Disgust: When you are disgusted, you might feel like you want to throw up. This emotion can happen when someone does something that's super gross. It can also happen when you see or smell something that stinks.

YOUR FEELINGS AND EMOTIONS MATTER

Some of us have difficulty accepting that our emotions are important. We're concerned about how others see us. We are worried that they will not like, approve of, or comprehend us.

Some of us do not regard ourselves highly enough to recognize the significance of our feelings. Many of us believe we are undeserving of certain things, which makes feeling and expressing certain feelings difficult.

Furthermore, we are often trained to prioritize the needs and feelings of others over our own. We suppose our feelings are useless because we are not given suitable ways for recognizing them.

Always remember to respect yourself and your feelings. When we don't respect ourselves, our feelings, or our emotions, we hurt ourselves by undervaluing ourselves. When we build a wall between ourselves and the rest of the world, we don't appreciate ourselves. We have difficulty expressing ourselves and assume that our emotions are insignificant.

KNOW WHAT MAKES YOU HAPPY

We all want to become happier. But what does that mean? Happier is when your feelings become more positive. For example, imagine you're learning to play ping pong. You start out and think, "I stink at this." You feel terrible. But you practice some more, and then you think, "Wow, I'm getting better." You feel hopeful. You became happier too.

Happiness happens all the time. It can be when you watch your favorite TV show or when you help plan your family's vacation to the Grand Canyon. It is the little and big moments where you feel better than before. Your mood improves—and the neat thing is, this can happen no matter how you were feeling before. Maybe you were feeling good, and now you feel great! Or maybe you were feeling angry, and now you feel just a little annoyed; that's also an improvement!

Feeling happier can happen when challenging things go away too. Maybe your teacher cancels the math test. Yay! Or the mean bully moves away, and no one picks on you. What a relief! Any thought or feeling that moves you in a more positive direction can help you become happier.

Sometimes becoming happier is complex too. Here are some additional things that can help move you in a happier direction:

- Helping others
- Thinking about challenges differently
- Using your unique talents
- Making friends

Shortly, we'll discuss these other ways of feeling good and becoming happier too. But let's not forget—becoming happier relies heavily on your skills as the captain of your emotional boat. The better you feel, the better you do.

Almost everyone on the planet has a "happy place" where they go because it helps them feel happier. It may be playing in the waves at the beach or sitting in your beanbag chair reading your favorite book. Doing something you enjoy or thinking something positive can also help you become happier.

Complete the following sentences to describe your happy place. There are no wrong answers.

My happy place is _____

In my happy place, I love to _____

My happy person or pet is _____

Other happy things I do are _____

Ways to Make Yourself Happier

Practice Gratitude

Gratitude moves us toward happier experiences, every single time. We may be feeling angry, sad, or disappointed, but if we can find something—anything—to be grateful for, our mood improves. Happier experiences can happen.

Gratitude helps us become happier. Of course, there are moments when we feel like things aren't going our way. Maybe you step in dog doo-doo or forget to bring your homework to school for the 100th time. You may even say it's a bad day. But even on no-good, rotten days, you can likely find something to feel thankful about, such as:

- You're listening to the birds chirp outside.
- The sun is shining.
- You get to play basketball today.

Gratitude helps you focus on the good things—the things that, even on challenging days, help you feel thankful. The more thankful you can feel even when things are challenging, the easier it is to turn your emotional boat around and sail through the choppy waters of life.

Gratitude is the feeling of being thankful. It's not saying "thank you" without thinking—it's really experiencing the feeling. Gratitude is the recognition that even on days that aren't perfect, there are people, places, and things that you are deeply thankful for (don't forget yourself).

List three things that you're grateful for at this moment:

1.

2.

3.

Showing your gratitude is called appreciation. If you have ever written a thank-you note, you have appreciated someone else and what they have done for you or given to you. Here are some different ways that you can show appreciation for others. Put a checkmark on the ones that you could do.

Be Optimistic

Optimism is looking on the bright side of life. Imagine it is raining. An optimist might say, "Awesome. I get to wear my new rain boots and splash in the puddles!" They are focusing on what feels good (positive) and choosing not to focus on the challenging (negative) part of the experience or situation.

Some days are clunkers. They just feel no good. That's normal, and you can often begin again, as we learned before. But the person who can see the positives in a negative situation is an optimist. Of course, some people are more optimistic than others, but everyone can get better at choosing to see the good things even when they're facing challenges.

Optimism is choosing to focus on the positive parts of any situation. Optimism isn't wimpy either. It takes a whole lot of courage to be optimistic in a world that often shares bad news, what you're doing wrong, and what you need to improve.

Optimistic people (both adults and children) are happier people. They see the good things, especially when others see challenges. Of course, they have challenging days too. But in general, optimistic people choose to ask: What good can come from this? Can I learn something here? What is my next best step?

Habits are the daily things we do. For example, you likely brush your teeth every day, and that helps you feel good and take care of your body. The same is true for your mind. You need to get into the habit of feeding it positive things every day to help it see the good things.

One way to become more optimistic is to look for positive things happening right now—things you can appreciate and focus on. For example, you might say, "I ate pizza today" or "I have no homework today!"

Make a list of three good things that happened today. There are no wrong answers.

1.

2.

3.

Identifying three good things from each day will help you become more optimistic, and it ultimately moves you in a happier direction. If it's been a challenging day and it's hard to find good things, the secret is to go back to the basics and be thankful for everything. For example: "I woke up today (a first good thing), my dog loves me (a second good thing), and the weekend is almost here (a third good thing)."

Helping Others

Helping others helps you become happier. Whether you help your family cook dinner, walk the dog, or tutor your friend, using your talents and energy to help others moves you in a positive-feeling direction too.

Opportunities to help others do and feel better are everywhere. You probably have heard of the "buddy bench" at some schools. It is a bench placed in the recess area, and if a student feels lonely, they can sit there. By sitting there, the student is saying, "Hi, I would like a friend," and naturally other students go over to help that student feel better and be their buddy.

Buddy benches have encouraged students to be kind to one another. Every little act of kindness is important; there is no act of helping that is too small. Even rescuing a bug (that has feelings) and putting it in a place that's better for it to live is bringing that bug benefit. Of course, you need to be careful to not get bitten or stung by harmful bugs either.

Helping others can take many forms. There is no limit to whom you can help, whether it's a person, an animal, a plant, or even the whole planet! We must do what we can to help every living creature live a happier life.

For now, let's focus on how you can help others this week. Place a checkmark on the activities you can do.

_____Use encouraging words, like "You've got this," "Way to go," and "You can do this!"

_____Teach someone something.

_____Do chores at home (take out the garbage, fold laundry, clean your room, etc.).

_____Hold doors open for people.

_____Compliment others.

_____Offer to help someone (maybe someone who is elderly or not tech savvy).

_____Listen to someone fully.

_____Tell a joke to help someone laugh.

The point is that as you help others become happier, you feel useful and usually become happier too. This is not helping that's forced. It's helping from the bottom of your heart—you truly want someone to struggle less and feel joy more.

Reframe Challenges

We all face challenges. Although challenges are hard, they help us appreciate when things feel easier and smoother. Every challenge can teach us something (like how to be patient or brave), and we can use it as a step toward happier life experiences.

Challenges can be big or small. A big challenge might be when your best friend moves away unexpectedly. A smaller challenge might be when you stub your toe on the foot of the couch—ouch! As we grow, what seems like a big challenge at one point soon becomes something we can handle, which makes it smaller. This is how life goes.

Challenges, like emotions, sometimes have speed. They can happen quickly, like when your teacher announces that you're having a surprise test. Others take time, like when you're hiking up a mountain, and it's only after you've done five miles that the hike starts to seem like a big challenge. Whether a challenge is big or small, fast or slow, it's an opportunity to learn and to keep moving toward happier life experiences.

Learning how to face a challenge and see the upside of it (if there is one) is helpful. Take, for example, the hike where after five miles, you're exhausted. Instead of complaining about hiking up the mountain with your family, you could instead think: "Wow, I am outside in nature hearing the birds. My body is tired, but this is good exercise. I will sleep well tonight!"

Changing how you see the situation (which is called "reframing") can help you feel better than before and make you feel strong as you set out on your path.

Challenges come in all shapes and sizes. Some common challenges are listed here. Circle the ones that you've experienced (whether recently or a long time ago).

- Being teased
- Forgetting your homework
- Getting punished
- Going to the hospital
- Stepping in dog poop
- Failing a test
- Losing a game
- Breaking something by accident
- Falling in front of others

Chances are good that you circled some of these challenges. The next step is to take one of these challenges (or another one that you think of) and find the positive parts of the experience. For example, if you keep forgetting your homework, maybe it's an opportunity to get more organized—so you decide to buy a special folder, make a checklist, and set an alarm every day to remind you! Pick a small challenge to start. Ask for help if needed.

What is your challenge? What is the upside? What good can come from this? What can you learn?

Make Friends

Having friends helps us become happier. They make us laugh, listen to us, and enjoy our company. Life without friends can feel lonely. Choosing our friends wisely is important because they become our extended family. People with friends are healthier and live longer too.

Friends are the sprinkles of life. They make everything more enjoyable and fun. You may have friends at school, in your neighborhood, on your sports team, or in your other activities. You can also make new friends throughout your life.

A real friend is nice to you, respects you, tells you the truth, is trustworthy, and might have similar interests as you. If someone isn't nice to you regularly, this person isn't your friend. Of course, a friend can have a bad day, but that doesn't happen often, and they apologize afterward.

Becoming a good friend is beneficial to everyone. You help others become happier, and you become happier too. There is no one on the planet who doesn't need a friend (even animals need friends!). Choosing your friends carefully is important, so let's talk more about what makes a good friend.

How do friends make you happier? Think of a friend you have now (or someone you had as a friend). Tell me how this relationship helped you. Furry friends count, too!

Name the friend:

- How long have you known this friend?
- What have you done together?
- How has this friend cheered you up?

- How does this friend make you laugh?
- How else does this friend make you happier?

THE EMOTIONS OF OTHER PEOPLE ARE ALSO IMPORTANT

When we talk about empathy, we mean the ability to identify with and comprehend the feelings of another individual. There are three main approaches to studying empathy.

Affective empathy is the first type of empathy. This is the ability to understand and sympathize with the feelings of others. People who, for example, have a strong bodily reaction after seeing a bad movie demonstrate that they are capable of affective empathy.

Cognitive empathy refers to a person's ability to comprehend another person's feelings. The psychologist who has a rational knowledge of the client's feelings but does not necessarily share the client's feelings viscerally is an excellent example of this.

Last but not least, emotional regulation is critical. This term refers to a person's capacity to manage their emotions. Maintaining emotional control is critical for surgeons, for example, while doing surgery on a patient.

Why Do We Need It?

Empathy is vital because it allows us to understand what other people are going through and respond appropriately.

Empathy is often connected with social interaction, and a large body of evidence suggests that higher degrees of empathy are associated with higher levels of altruistic conduct.

There are situations, however, when this is not the case. Empathy can restrict social behavior and even lead to immoral behavior in certain persons. For example, a person who witnesses a car accident and is overcome with emotion when seeing the sufferer in excruciating pain is less likely to help that person. People are less likely to give aid in this situation.

Having strong empathetic feelings for members of our own family, social or cultural group can lead to hatred or violence toward those we perceive as a danger to us. Consider a mother or father defending their kid or a patriot defending their country. Both are motivated by a desire to help their respective causes.

Con artists, fortune tellers, and psychics, who are adept at understanding other people's emotions, may be able to exploit their empathic abilities to promote their aims by fooling others.

FIVE WAYS TO READ OTHER PEOPLE'S EMOTIONS

1. Recognize and accept your feelings.

Recognize and accept your emotions as they arise. Your feelings may reveal a lot about your attitude and how you behave.

You will be more aware of the variables that contribute to constructing your feelings if you can name them as they occur.

Examine your feelings when you cannot move, such as while sitting at a meeting. Pay attention to how you respond emotionally when someone compliments you on a job well done.

When you have a thorough grasp of your own emotions, you can discern them in others. It is also a lot easier for you to pick up on other people's emotions and mental states.

2. Make an effort to get along with others around you.

It is much easier to read someone if you already have a relationship with them.

More people will come toward you if you are friendly and have an open mind. They relax and let down their guard when they are with you because they are at ease.

Empathy will help you to understand what other people are going through. It will be a lot simpler for you to actively listen to what they have to say after you've experienced what they're going through.

When you have a true connection with others, you will notice that you can sense both your own and their energy.

3. Be aware of your body language

Your body language is a physical expression of your emotions.

If you are scared, you may begin to sweat. When you're under a lot of stress, your nerves may catch up with you.

This is because your body and mind are not two distinct things but one interconnected totality. They cooperate.

When you've mastered your body language signals, you'll be able to detect comparable clues in the body language of others very instantly.

You may tell a lot about someone's body language by looking at their body. Understanding what someone truly means by what they do can be challenging since individuals regularly say things that contradict how they truly feel.

4. Be objective

Every person is one-of-a-kind. Maintain objectivity in your approach while acknowledging and appreciating human variety.

It would help if you did not rely on your intuition or the innate information that your emotions carry.

Learning about a person is not the same as understanding that person. You must also consider the impact you make on other individuals.

Be mindful of how your words and actions impact the emotions of individuals around you, whether they are afraid, stupid, happy, or glad.

You can see if you set aside your own beliefs, thoughts, and prejudices. Also, if anything has to be repaired, ensure it is done.

5. Have faith in yourself

You may find it easy to distinguish the sensation in your tummy after you have been entirely attuned to yourself.

Your intuition is rarely wrong, and the messages it sends may have a precise reason. It is trustworthy and dependable.

Emotional intelligence may be developed with a lot of practice and hard effort. It will all be worthwhile in the end, especially if you can rapidly distinguish the energy and thoughts of individuals around you who are also doing this.

2

THE BENEFITS OF SOCIALIZING THE RIGHT WAY

Socializing, simply put, is interacting with others. Because these skills will be useful to your child for the rest of his or her life, it's vital to begin developing them at a young age so that connections can be made. When it comes to a child's mental, physical, and emotional health, the consequences of ignoring the need to cultivate socializing cannot be overstated.

WHY IS SOCIALIZING IMPORTANT?

Socializing your child at an early age is vital since it will help them build skills that will aid in their healthy growth and relationships, such as the ones listed below.

Helps Boost Communication Skills

Understanding and practicing communication skills will benefit your kid as they progress through life stages such as entering child care, starting school, or participating in sports and extracurricular activities (Pescaru, 2018). Allowing children to speak with people outside of their immediate family encourages them to learn about risk-taking, social cues, and how to listen and comprehend others. It's also worth noting that communication abilities can take many forms, including nonverbal and vocal communication, such as chattiness, interest, and hand gestures. So don't be concerned if your youngster isn't as talkative as the person next to them.

Improves Confidence

Socializing encourages children to develop skills that will help them become self-assured and independent later in life. Social contacts will help youngsters grow their self-esteem and resilience in the face of the unfamiliar, resulting in connections that make new social encounters less frightening. Because school might be a huge and intimidating new setting for your child, this is an especially crucial ability on the first day of school. Your child will be more inclined to take healthy risks, such as swimming or chatting to someone new, if they have resilience and confidence.

Helps You Learn to Share

Children learn to share and become less egocentric as a result of socialization. Egocentrism is a common trait among young children, especially first- or only-borns, since their minds are preoccupied with what they can see rather than what they can't see or envision. Children who socialize are more likely to interact with others and share resources and information. They are beginning to comprehend the notion of others by sharing their information, experiences, and resources, which will help them with creative and logical thinking later in life. Sharing and socializing also help children (and adults) create friends, which is crucial for a child's emotional and mental well-being.

Develops Empathy

Socializing your child exposes them to new ideas, thoughts, and distinctions but also aids in developing empathy. Empathy is crucial because it helps youngsters be nice and compassionate to others. As previously said, socializing entails not just talking but also listening, observing, and reacting. Seeing someone aiding someone hurting or standing up to others for being mistreated teaches a crucial lesson in empathy that can only be learned via social interaction. Empathetic children will be more welcoming, open, and resilient in the future since they have learned how to deal with conflict, communicate, and successfully adapt to new surroundings.

Helps You Make Friends

Finally, socialization is critical in assisting your youngster in making friends. Friendships are beneficial for various reasons, including expanding your child's language, forming bonds that foster alternative ways of thinking, and generating lifetime memories for you and your child. Friends are a network of people outside of your immediate family who can aid and encourage your child through difficult times in their life, such as starting school, participating in sports or extracurricular activities, or performing in their first recital. Because your child feels supported, they might become thrilled about big occasions when their friends are engaged. At all phases of life, friends are the foundation of our social network and may help us decrease stress and enhance our mental and physical well-being.

Socialization Has Health Benefits

You've probably heard that "humans are a sociable species" and that socializing offers many benefits. You may have experienced these benefits yourself. It's nice to laugh with someone, share an inside joke, and know you have someone to talk to when you have a problem.

But what evidence does science have for the psychological and physical benefits of social contact? What can we learn from studies to help us thrive? How can social interaction increase our well-being, and what can we learn from research to help us feel well? Here are a few health benefits.

Socializing Boosts Immunity

Through inflammatory reactions, your immune system helps defend your body from foreign infections (such as bacteria and viruses) and physical harm. These bodily reactions, such as an increased need for sleep and changes in food, can be triggered by stress.

Several studies of individuals with various conditions have found that social support can help them heal and operate better. For example, more social support has enhanced breast cancer survival rates (Reblin & Uchino, 2008).

Interactions aren't enough to protect you from sickness; the quality of your relationships is crucial. One research looked at the interactions of 42 married couples aged 22 to 77 (Soulsby & Bennett, 2015). The researchers discovered that when couples had disagreements, wound healing was slower than when they had social support contacts. Couples with high levels of conflict and hostility healed at 60% of the rate of couples with low levels of hostility.

Studies show that stress, especially social stress, can harm our immune system. Increased social engagement can protect against the disease since loneliness and isolation can be substantial sources of stress. On the other hand, loneliness is caused by a lack of social engagements and a lack of rewarding social relationships.

As a result, it's advisable to avoid people who criticize you and make you feel bad about yourself.

Socializing Lowers Your Risk of Dementia

Alzheimer's disease and other kinds of dementia can be reduced by socializing. According to research, loneliness (how socially isolated someone feels) and poor social engagement (measured by limited social circles, married status, and social activities) are linked to an increased risk of Alzheimer's disease (Waterstone on Augusta, 2018)

For seniors who have already developed dementia, shared meals and support groups have been advocated as ways to increase social connection. Supporting caretakers can enhance the quality of care, and social interactions for persons living with dementia by enhancing the quality of the caretaker-patient connection since carers for loved ones with dementia have greater rates of depression than their peers.

Using technology, social events, and other types of engagement to assist seniors in maintaining social connections in retirement can help them maintain their physical and mental health for longer.

Socializing Improves Brain Health and Performance

We use regions of our brains that are also critical for remembering and solving rational issues and puzzles when we socialize. Other activities we often conceive of as "intellectually stimulating," such as puzzles, riddles, or word games, may work our minds just as effectively as social engagement.

One researcher looked at persons aged 24 to 96 and discovered that social connection and involvement had a favorable impact on cognitive performance at all ages. The most positive finding of their research was that even 10 minutes of social engagement was adequate to improve cognitive performance in terms of working memory and processing speed, (Cohut, 2018).

Because our brain is in charge of our entire body, improving our brain health through more social engagement can only benefit our overall health.

Socializing Promotes Mental Health

Socializing can aid in the reduction of depression, anxiety, and other mental health conditions, as well as stabilize emotions.

Several studies have found a correlation between loneliness and depression, with individuals with stronger social contacts having a lower risk of sadness (Brody, 2017).

Depending on how it is used, social media appears to have both beneficial and harmful effects on mental health. According to one study, using social media sites for positive interactions and social support was associated with lower levels of anxiety and depression, (Seabrook et al., 2016). Negative connections and social comparison on social media, on the other hand, were associated with greater levels of despair and anxiety.

Increasing social support can help people with depression feel better. Peer support groups were shown to be just as beneficial as conventional therapies like CBT in treating depression in one research on cognitive-behavioral therapy (NHS, 2021).

WORKBOOK QUESTIONS FOR SELF-REFLECTION ABOUT SOCIALIZATION

Recall a time when you shared someone else's concern. How did it feel?

……………………………………………………………………

Have you ever said hello to someone before? Say something about the experience

……………………………………………………………………

Having trouble meeting new people? If so, why do you believe that?

……………………………………………………………………

Have you recently made friends? How do you feel when you are with each other?

……………………………………………………………………

3

GIVE FIRST: EMPATHY AND COMPASSION

How would you feel if your friends or family members just looked at you and walked away every time you cried or felt sad? Research shows that today's kids are 40% less emphatic than 30 years ago!

Empathy is simply being sensitive to other people's feelings. For example, a child becomes aware of the other child's emotions and tries to avoid hurting him because he now thinks about how his friend is feeling. After understanding how the other child feels, you have to show them that you care by helping them. You can talk to them, hug them, or change how you normally behave before you understand what they are going through.

This chapter discusses how children should learn to give empathy and compassion to others.

ADDRESSING YOUR DOUBTS

Why Do I Find it Hard to Socialize and Talk to Others?

Feeling self-conscious, apprehensive, or shy is normal when you're in front of people. Most individuals manage to get through these times when they need to. However, the anxiety that comes with being shy or self-conscious can overwhelm some people.

It's probably more than shyness when people are so self-conscious and worried that they avoid speaking out or socializing with others most of the time. It might be a social phobia, which is an anxiety disorder also called social anxiety.

What happens when someone has a social phobia? Extreme shyness and self-consciousness morph into a terrifying fear. As a result, a person feels uneasy in social situations regularly. People who suffer from social anxiety typically find it easy to engage with their family and a few close friends. Meeting new people, conversing in a group, or speaking in public, on the other hand, might trigger their acute shyness. People with social phobia may fear social events rather than enjoy them and may even avoid some of them entirely.

How Do I Know People Will Want to Talk to Me?

When you're preparing to approach someone, look for the following signs to see if they want to chat with you.

Do they return your smile?

If you're a shy person, this one's for you. Has someone across the packed room been staring at you? Smile and observe what happens if your eyes connect. If the individual grins back, it indicates that they're interested in talking to you. Smiling is a generally recognized gesture as a prelude to "hello."

Make sure you're making eye contact with the person you're interested in and not staring them down with aggressive eyes.

Are they leaning in your direction?

You may be surrounded by other individuals depending on what social context you are in. Someone on the periphery of your conversation or group could lean in closer. Humans are social creatures, and they almost always want to be involved.

Perhaps you're in a coffee shop, and you're alone. If someone is sitting close to you and leaning in, you might interpret this as a subconscious indicator that they want to talk to you.

Our body does not deceive us. If someone approaches you, don't hesitate to speak up and initiate a discussion. They're probably waiting for you to do just that.

Are their feet pointing towards you?

Have you ever heard the phrase, "If someone is interested in you, they will point their feet in your direction while you are speaking?"

This is an old ploy, but the adage has some truth. Take a minute to look down if you're in the thick of a discussion. What is the orientation of your feet, and where are the other persons?

If they're pointing at you, that's a good indication. It's also a good indicator if they're pointed in the same direction as your feet. It might be mirroring, which I discuss further down, or they wish to proceed in the same direction as you. If they're pointing away from you or in a location where your feet aren't, it clearly indicates that they're ready to finish the conversation.

Are they mirroring you?

Keep an eye on your physical body while you're speaking. Your hand motions and posture may be reflected back at you. Research has shown that we become copycats when we are attracted to another individual.

We can't help ourselves; we want to do everything we can to reassure the other person that we want to stay in their company and value what they offer. It's a means for us to express our desire to connect. On the other hand, if you're making hand motions and the other person crosses their arms, especially if their feet are pointing away, it might hint that they want to end the conversation.

Will Other Kids Reject Me?

Peer relationships are crucial, but they are not always positive. Children will learn a great deal from their connections, both positive and negative. It's here that they'll begin to form opinions about how the world will treat them, what the world will think of them if they are secure, whether people are safe, and how much power they own. It's also where they'll discover that "mean for no reason" exists, that people occasionally do things that make no sense, that individuals who treat them like rock stars are worth keeping, and that other people don't deserve to be around them.

Children may be outgoing and sympathetic, as well as mean and cruel, and all children will encounter both. The playground, understandably, may feel like the beginning and end of their universe. When they are rejected, it might feel as though the rest of the world consists of individuals who do not understand them.

Our children must understand that for every youngster that is mean, there will be many more who appreciate them for who they are. It's only a matter of identifying their tribe, which they'll all have. Finding friends, on the other hand, might be more difficult than it should be — and this is due to no fault of their own.

Understandably, rejection might seem personal to many youngsters. Every rejection has the potential to be devastating, but when it seems personal, it is even more so. We may explain, as many parents would, that the reasons for their exclusion have nothing to do with them, but children are curious and intelligent, and their open brains are eager to learn as much as possible. They're likely to think, 'Well, if they aren't rejecting me because of me, why are they rejecting me?'

How to Help a Child Overcome Rejection

It's critical to understand the reasons for rejection to assist your child in overcoming it. Once you've figured out what's causing the problem (via your child's reports, teacher conferences, and observation), you may start addressing it in the following ways:

- Assist your child in being aware of troublesome habits and working to eliminate them (thumb sucking, nose picking, scribbling out answers or ideas, attention-seeking or boasting).
- Praise your youngster when you notice them engaging in socially beneficial conduct and explain why the activity was appropriate.
- Teach your youngster how to ask and answer questions, give and take turns speaking, and bring up subjects of mutual interest.

- Work with your child to identify their abilities and interests and then capitalize on them by participating in afterschool or community activities. Activities that increase confidence, such as martial arts, might be very beneficial
- Discuss with your child how close relationships are far more significant than popularity and how they can develop the potential ties they already have.

When your child is feeling rejected, pay attention to them. Knowing they have unwavering love and support at home might help him or her feel more confident.

FEEL WHAT OTHERS FEEL

Learning to Give Empathy to Others

Empathy is an important component of healthy friendships and relationships. It lowers conflict and misunderstandings and promotes helpful conduct, compassion, and overall life success.

Empathy may be taught and developed in youngsters, just like any other talent. The most successful tactics to use depend on the child's age because cognitive capacities and life experiences improve throughout time.

Let's take a look at some fundamental tactics for teaching children at any age empathy.

Demonstrate empathy.

When teaching a youngster a new ability, it's critical to set an example for them. This enables the youngster to comprehend what empathy looks, sounds, and feels like. It's also simpler to teach a talent that you've previously mastered.

Even when you're angry with or punishing your child, remember to display empathy. This emphasizes the need of using empathy even when you're dissatisfied, wounded, or furious. The more empathy a youngster receives, the more likely they are to extend it to others.

Discuss emotions.

Rather than ignoring or hiding feelings, talk about them honestly. Let's assume your youngster is afraid of the dark. Rather than replying, "There's nothing to be afraid of," inquire about the child's concerns: "Are you afraid of the dark?" What frightens you about the dark?"

If your child doesn't like another child, don't say, "That's wrong," but rather inquire as to why the youngster feels that way. This might lead to a conversation regarding the activities of the other kid and why the child is acting the way he or she is (e.g., They just relocated to a new school and are feeling sad because they miss their old school and their friends).

Never scold or chastise a youngster who is unhappy or angry. Make it obvious that all emotions are acceptable, and through conversation and reflection, teach them to regulate them in a healthy way.

Volunteer at home, in the neighborhood, or on a worldwide scale.

Assisting others in developing kindness and compassion. It can also allow children to engage with individuals from all origins, ages, and circumstances, making it simpler for them to express empathy for others.

Read through our list of activities that make a difference at home, in the community, and across the world, then choose one or two to begin with.

Recognize and reward empathic behavior.

Praise your youngster when he or she demonstrates empathy for others. Emphasizing and promoting compassionate conduct promote it in the future.

Make the compliment specific: "You gave your sister a Band-Aid to help her feel better after she scraped her knee." That was really thoughtful and helpful!"

COMPASSION FOR OTHERS

What is Compassion?

Compassion entails empathizing with another person's suffering and wanting to assist in relieving it. It is similar to other emotions like sympathy, empathy, and altruism, yet some important distinctions exist between the concepts. Empathy refers to the ability to see things from another person's point of view and to experience other people's feelings. Compassion, on the other hand, happens when empathy is combined with a desire to assist others.

How to Learn Compassion as a Young Adult

I've listed eight techniques to assist your child, or student develop compassion as a character trait and a behavioral style in the following sections:

Be an example to others.

Children may pay attention to what you say but learn more from what they see. When you get the opportunity to perform a random act of compassion, please take advantage of it! When you're dissatisfied in a social situation, communicate your anger in words that respect the dignity of the person you're speaking with. Stop what you're doing and help someone who needs it, even (read: especially!) if it's not convenient for you. Remember that opportunities to express compassion do not present themselves on a schedule. Demonstrate to young people that actions of service and compassion for others can be performed at any moment.

Empower the child by putting them on the receiving end of compassion.

While teaching a youngster to exhibit compassion to others is a good start, allowing a young person to feel compassion firsthand is much more powerful. If your child is wounded or ill, give them enough TLCC (tender, loving, compassionate care.) It may seem self-evident, but responding to a youngster when he is sad or sick is the most effective method to teach him compassion for others.

Speak your mind

Most children may learn about real compassion by witnessing and experiencing it in action, but when parents talk about acts of compassion openly, they transmit the significance of compassion as a treasured family value. As you and your child watch TV or movies together, point out situations where compassion was exhibited — or should have been expressed! Talk about individuals who need compassion the most, such as the elderly and children who are poor.

Volunteer Your Time

When youngsters participate actively in acts of compassion for others, they learn about this virtue in a profound and lasting way. Find age-appropriate activities to introduce your youngster to volunteering. These activities are both important and enjoyable, making them particularly successful in getting children to think compassionately about the needs of others regularly.

Take Care of a Pet

Bringing a pet into a family is not a decision to be made lightly or rashly, but it is worthwhile to give serious thought to giving your child the experience of caring for an animal as a method to promote compassion. Children who look after dogs acquire valuable lessons such as responsibility, unconditional love, empathy, and compassion for all living creatures.

You Can Show Love to Another Shy Kid

A child's shyness is understandable. It's very uncommon for youngsters to feel like they're on show, avoid meeting new people, or prefer sitting on the sidelines rather than being in the thick of the activity. However, there are certain things you can do to assist your child cope with their anxiety.

What Does Children's Shyness Look Like?

Children frequently experience anxiety when confronted with unfamiliar surroundings or individuals. Unfortunately, our culture frequently rewards extroverted types over introverted personalities, which can pressure children as they go through natural developmental stages. This might lead to feelings of self-consciousness in inherently introverted youngsters.

Some symptoms that your child's shyness harms them and that they may require assistance include:

- Reduced social skills or participation in socializing
- Fewer friends
- Less involvement in enriching activities like athletics, dancing, theatre, or music.
- Isolation, loneliness, insignificance, and self-consciousness are all common feelings.
- Unnecessary stress caused by other people's opinions limits your child's capacity to realize their full potential.
- High levels of anxiety
- Physical afflictions such as blushing, stammering, and trembling.

How to Help a Shy Child

While shyness is a normal developmental stage that your child will most likely outgrow, you may assist them by doing the following:

Never put a label on your child that says they are shy. If your child is aware of their shyness, they may begin to criticize themselves when they behave shyly. The notion that shyness is bad or indicates something is wrong with your child will only make them feel timider.

Accept your child as they are. Never make a joke about your child's shyness. Please make an effort to show them that you accept and adore them for who they are.

Make an effort to understand. Inquire about your child's timidity. Try to comprehend their apprehensions or reservations about revealing themselves to the rest of the world.

Discuss the advantages of being extroverted. Tell the child how being outgoing has benefited you in your life. Discuss the types of behaviors you'd like your youngster to adopt. When your child exhibits these characteristics, praise them.

Set goals. Set goals for your child to achieve to feel more comfortable socializing. Make sure your objectives are simple and attainable. It may be as simple as greeting one person each day.

Introduce your youngster to new experiences. Try to introduce your youngster to fresh experiences and show them new things. If they become more outgoing over time, be supportive of them.

Ensure your child can accomplish activities that they excel in. If your child can engage in things they enjoy and are competent at, they will get a strong feeling of purpose and self-assurance. When they are good at something, compliment them and allow them to do it. They may find it simpler to connect with youngsters who share similar interests if they participate in activities they like.

Standing Up for Others Is Being Compassionate

Some people are born with an uncontrollable need to serve others. Something inside them makes it unbearable for them to stand by and watch others suffer.

These people are born with compassion, altruism, empathy, and a constant awareness of others' needs. They can scarcely comprehend the world's brutal and violent past, but they are aware of humanity's often nasty impulses.

We live in a culture that promotes aggressive individuality, and many people try to live by the "survival of the fittest" philosophy. While self-sufficiency has its advantages, social relationships ultimately allow our species to thrive and flourish.

We must find a way to overcome society's growing skepticism and provide a helping hand when needed.

Compassion is a huge power that requires fortitude. It does not mean weakness or gullibility. Not to add, the interrelated nature of this perplexing universe necessitates that we are more kind.

All elements of our lives are connected with those of others, whether we like it or not. Humanity's fate is intertwined.

Please stand up for people in need; it's a selfless way of life that benefits everyone, including yourself. Compassion is a quality that elevates our entire species.

WORKBOOK QUESTIONS FOR COMPASSION AND EMPATHY IN YOUNG CHILDREN

Which decisions make you feel deeply uncomfortable?

……………………………………………………………

How do you strike a balance between your own wants and those of others?

……………………………………………………………

What methods do you use to console others?

……………………………………………………………

When did you feel the most compelled to be your best self?

……………………………………………………………

Is there ever a time when your curiosity gets the best of you?

……………………………………………………………

What do you want others to know about you?

……………………………………………………………

What are your coping mechanisms for bad emotions?

……………………………………………………………

4

WHEN YOU SEEM TO BE RUNNING OUT OF CONFIDENCE

Confidence is having faith in yourself, your talents, and your ideas. Examples include believing in one's ability to learn a new song for their band to play or being able to ask someone out without getting butterflies in the stomach.

Accepting and loving who you are as you are, whether that means being proud of your achievements or hair color, accepting that you're not very good at sports, or refusing to change who you are in order to fit in with others is part of being confident. Being outgoing does not equate to being confident. You can be quiet and still be confident.

WHY CONFIDENCE IS IMPORTANT IN SOCIALIZING

Confidence is the key to improving many elements of your life. It advances your career and supports the achievement of your daily goals.

Fast Company reported a study from Ohio State University (OSU) that found a correlation between employment trajectories and self-confidence. According to OSU, confidence necessitates ongoing revision and the ability to see several versions of oneself. As you gain confidence in your capacity to imagine yourself reaching your goal, your chances of success rise.

Establishing confidence is indeed challenging. In an interview with the BBC, Roy Baumeister of Florida State University discussed self-esteem and noted that confidence comes from having a supportive family and community. In reality, many individuals grow up and go on to live their lives without either. Some people must deal with their own self-esteem issues on their own.

Many people are unaware that you may gain confidence in social circumstances, which is when you need it the most. Confidence is the peak of your social talents, and it can only be gained via constant social engagement. The benefits of social involvement for self-esteem may be observed in a variety of ways.

According to Inc. Magazine, you may boost your self-esteem by teaching people about the sector in which you work. By doing this, you are reassuring yourself of your own talents and that you are more than capable of fulfilling tasks and goals. It's the best method for recognizing your worth, according to the magazine.

Receiving feedback, according to the Harvard Business Review, is another factor in increasing your confidence. You quickly overcome any uneasiness by asking for help from others. As a result of their compliments, you may feel validated and safe. On the other hand, input from others may assist you in being modest and grounded.

As you determine who to contact, you should be aware of the toxic people to avoid. This is one of The Bridgemaker's finest bits of advice for boosting self-confidence. Don't listen to those who make you feel bad about yourself since they might really make things worse by being negative influences. Others will always erode your confidence, no matter how long you have known someone. Their critique is typically unconstructive and scathing, which is a telltale sign. These comments are made by those who, in truth, lack confidence and are duped into believing that they can improve their own by insulting others.

If you start or continue to put these tips into action, you will automatically gain more self-worth and confidence. As a result, you will be able to live your life the way you want while also achieving your goals.

HOW DO YOU KNOW YOU LACK CONFIDENCE?

First off, it's crucial to understand that just because a child is quiet or introverted, it doesn't automatically follow that they have poor self-esteem. The contrary is frequently possible.

Everybody occasionally experiences self-doubt or confidence setbacks. This is quite typical. However, if your child exhibits chronic symptoms of poor self-esteem, this may be an indication that they are having difficulties and require further care.

So what exactly are the most telling signs that a child lacks confidence? Let me list some of the most typical warning signs.

- Discussing oneself in an extremely bad light, like saying, "I'm unattractive," "I'm dumb."
- Constantly making harsh comparisons to others.
- Worrying about what other people think of them.
- Mood swings, frequently seeming melancholy, withdrawn, furious, or sad. Losing their temper easily and being easily moved to tears.
- Will frequently go to great measures to avoid social events since they don't have many friends or prefer to be alone themselves.
- Considering their efforts to never be as effective as those of others.

- Finding it challenging to accept compliments or criticism.
- A fear of failure that prevents them from attempting new things.
- Saying "I can't" and giving up readily.
- Finding it difficult to deal with failure.
- If they believe they are about to lose a game, lying or cheating.
- They could attempt to minimize the significance of activities in which they abstain, saying things such as, "I didn't want to be in the play anyhow."
- A decline of interest in previously enjoyed activities.
- Deterioration in their academic performance.
- Engaging in bad behaviors including skipping class, smoking, drinking, or generally acting out.

BUILDING CONFIDENCE IN YOURSELF STEP BY STEP

It might take time and effort to develop your confidence. Furthermore, what helps you now could not benefit you in the future. However, there are many things you can do to boost your confidence in your skills and self-perception.

Be Kind to Yourself

Recognize and resist your unkind thoughts. Talk to yourself like you would a close friend to try to accomplish this. How may someone else view this? Is there anything that implies this might not occur? You could think more logically and calmly after responding to these questions.

Keep in mind that it's okay to make mistakes. When you do make a mistake, it's crucial to accept responsibility for it.

Do not compare yourself to others. Consider the fact that people carefully select or filter the images they post on social media. Additionally, they frequently fail to depict how people's real lives are.

Repeat positive statements to yourself. For example, you may say 'I am enough' or 'I am worth it' to yourself in the mirror every morning.

Look after Yourself

Try to get enough sleep, eat a healthy diet, remain active, spend time in nature, and refrain from using drugs and alcohol.

Focus on the Positives

You might acknowledge your accomplishments. Additionally, you may compile a list of your positive traits so you can review them in the future. This could apply to any praises you receive, even if you don't first believe them. You could start to develop a new perspective on yourself over time.

Spend Time with People

Have fun with your loved ones, make connections with those you trust and identify with, and show them some kindness. These are the individuals who will accept you just as you are.

You may boost your self-esteem by volunteering, lending a hand, or using your abilities to assist a friend or family member.

Do Things You Enjoy

This might be everything from swimming to playing video games to music listening. Even if it's just for a few minutes, allow yourself to enjoy yourself guilt-free.

Act Confident when You Don't Feel It

To build up acting confident in front of people, you may begin by practicing conversing or a posture in front of a mirror. However, if you can maintain it, you can discover after some time that you're not acting anymore.

Try Something New

You may learn a skill and meet new people by trying something new. It can involve picking up a few new words in a foreign tongue, mastering a musical instrument, creating art through painting or drawing, or signing up for a class or sports team. You might do it for fun or set objectives for yourself to see how you progress.

WORKBOOK QUESTIONS FOR IMPROVING CONFIDENCE FOR KIDS

Children may develop their confidence in amazing ways by asking questions. Good questions get kids to pause and reflect. Thus they are effective to consider. Take a moment to reflect on their life and the world around them. Children naturally ask questions. Therefore, why not take advantage of that interest while you try to strengthen their self-esteem and leadership abilities?

How can we help kids develop their confidence? By asking them questions, you may guide your kids' development toward being outstanding leaders and people.

Would you kindly illustrate something you do well?

....

What do your friends think of you?

....

What sets you apart?

....

Let's build a list of the top 10 skills you have. Which one of them inspires you the most, and why?

....

How did you assist someone today?

....

I love how you support our family. What do you consider to be some of your most important contributions?

....

What do you believe they are currently feeling?

....

How can they apologize when they know they have wounded someone?

....

Have you ever experienced something similar to this? What did you do to address the issue at hand?

....

5

NON-VIOLENT COMMUNICATION (NVC)

Today, being able to communicate well orally might be considered a necessary life skill. Early on, parents should begin teaching their children the fundamentals of communication, and as the child becomes older, they should seek to improve those abilities. It might be a grievous mistake to assume that children will pick up appropriate communication skills on their own. Parents now teach their children how to speak respectfully in addition to successfully.

WHY IS COMMUNICATION SKILLS DEVELOPMENT IMPORTANT FOR CHILDREN?

Children that are taught excellent communication techniques are better able to express themselves and communicate their emotions.

Learning and meaningful information exchange with others can be facilitated by effective communication skills.

A youngster who is proficient in verbal communication may also feel at ease writing, which will likely improve his or her academic performance.

Children who struggle with language development may go on to have behavioral disorders like depression, social disengagement, and low self-esteem.

HOW CAN I HELP MY CHILD TO COMMUNICATE EFFECTIVELY?

To the best of your ability, try to comprehend what your youngster is trying to say. How does your child express their hunger or fatigue? How do they communicate their desires for or against physical contact?

Even before they are able to comprehend what you are saying, you should talk to newborns. Watch your youngster jabber back at you while you talk to them about what you are doing. Together with your child, sing lullabies and nursery rhymes. Your child's linguistic skills can be developed through rhyme and rhythm.

As kids become older, they learn how to write basic texts to communicate thoughts, messages, emotions, and facts. As adolescents mature, they usually become more adept in connecting concepts in a variety of ways and planning artwork that conveys ideas, thoughts, observations, feelings, and experiences.

Demonstrate great communication by talking to your child and listening to what they have to say. Make an effort to ask questions that don't only need a "yes" or "no" answer.

Play activities with the words and sounds and read stories to your youngster.

Create basic books, signs, and posters (either manually or using a computer) if your youngster is interested in words and letters. To help you create a text message, letter, or email, ask your youngster for advice. Type their name for them. Find letters on the keyboard to play games.

With your child, read from books, periodicals, billboards, advertising, and photographs. Help children recognize words and letters, as well as the way that images may convey information. Discuss what you see, the meaning of the text, and the images.

Encourage your youngster to tell you stories by telling them to you.

You can tell these stories in your native tongue in addition to (or instead of) English.

TYPES OF COMMUNICATION I NEED TO KNOW

There are five main types of communication, namely, verbal communication, non-verbal communication, visual communication, written communication, and listening.

Verbal Communication

This type of communication involves exchanging information orally and through sign language. Many people use this kind of communication, including one-on-one meetings, phone calls, video conferences, and presentations. Verbal communication is important since it is productive and successful.

Nonverbal Communication

Facial expressions, hand gestures, and body language are examples of non-verbal communication. It could be accidental or deliberate. For instance, you could unconsciously smile when you come across any delightful, pleasing, and intriguing information. When attempting to comprehend the emotions and feelings of others, it is highly beneficial.

Visual Communication

Information may be shared visually by using graphs, charts, sketches, drawings, artwork, and pictures. By providing context to their written or spoken material, people employ pictures to complement their presentation. The audience may absorb concepts and information more readily while communicating visually, which is a beneficial learning technique.

Written Communication

The exchange of information using written words, printed and typed symbols, numbers, and letters is known as written communication. It's significant since it provides valuable information for documentation and reference. Memos, letters, blogs, essays, pamphlets, and novels are just a few media that individuals use to disseminate written information. Emails and charts are two more typical professional communication tools.

Listening

Without listening, communication cannot be completed; listening concentrates on what you do while you are not speaking. Listening is the most challenging and important aspect of communication. However, you shouldn't only concentrate on hearing what the other person is saying when you're speaking with them. Instead, it would be best if you focused on the speakers' nonverbal clues and their overall communication, such as their fidgeting and toying with their hands and other objects while they speak.

WHAT IS NONVIOLENT COMMUNICATION?

Also called compassionate communication, nonviolent communication (NVC) aims to improve our capacity to elicit compassion from others and to demonstrate compassion toward ourselves. By concentrating our attention on what we are observing, experiencing, requiring, and requesting, NVC helps us to rethink how we communicate with and hear others.

We are taught to make thoughtful, unevaluated observations and to identify the situations and behaviors that influence us. We develop the ability to recognize and clearly express our desires at any given time as well as our deeper needs and those of others. We learn the extent of our own compassion when we put more of our attention on defining what is being seen, felt, and required than on labeling and judging. NVC encourages respect, attentiveness, and empathy via its emphasis on deep listening—to oneself as well as to others—and engenders a shared desire to offer from the heart. The form is straightforward but incredibly transformational.

HOW LEARNING NONVIOLENT COMMUNICATE WILL HELP ME

Let's look at three instances when young people may use this approach to talk to their parents about common conflicts.

Example: Disagreements over education and future prospects

Emma is seventeen years old and getting ready to apply to college. She's always been a voracious reader and wants to focus on English literature. Her parents, however, believe it is unrealistic. They want her to focus on a subject like business or economics that is more practical. How should she approach them about this?

Emma understands she will have to spend the next three years studying whichever topic she picks, making the issue challenging. She knows her interest in English and how much she would like to study it. Her parents are worried about how effectively her degree would prepare her for the future and her employment chances.

Emma would communicate poorly if she became enraged and told her parents she didn't care what they thought. Even if the statements are accurate, saying things like "You don't understand me" or "You want to control everything I do" won't help Emma obtain what she wants.

Emma can instead use the plan we outlined and say:

"You are aware of my lifelong passion for reading. Books have heavily influenced my life."

She could describe your feelings as follows: "I feel happy and optimistic when I think of studying English. I get restless and uninspired when I consider learning something else."

She could express understanding for her parents' concerns by saying, "I know you're worried about my future, and you want me to be able to acquire a decent job after my studies are up."

Finally, she could offer a compromise: "What if I majored in English and took some business classes too? I could then be motivated by my academics while simultaneously honing my talents for potential employment."

HOW TO START AND CARRY ON A CONVERSATION

Starting a conversation with a stranger might be frightening. Here's how to carry on a conversation like a pro to assist you in creating those crucial relationships.

What Makes a Good Conversation?

Many components make for a great discussion. Here are some of the factors that can prevent uncomfortable silences.

1. Active listening

Active listening focuses on paying attention to what is being said when someone is speaking. Sometimes people listen to respond to what their conversation partner is saying instead of hearing what they are saying.

If you employ this key tactic, your discussion partner will be aware that you are paying close attention. Furthermore, you'll probably remember more of the conversation afterward. By speaking less and listening more, repeating what you've just heard back to the speaker, and engaging in active listening, you may improve your listening abilities.

2. Asking and answering questions

Asking questions is another technique to demonstrate that you are a good listener.

The conversation can be extended by asking questions about what the other person stated. Or you might enquire about anything you weren't entirely clear on or are eager to learn more about.

Once more, this demonstrates to the other person that you are genuinely interested in what they say.

3. Discovering shared hobbies and characteristics

Listen carefully throughout conversations to find experiences that you both share. You may keep the conversation running organically by bringing up mutual interests, which will offer you something to chat about.

Finding commonalities will help you start a discussion and make it more fruitful. This is important for maintaining the flow of discourse.

4. Having an intention for the conversation

Having a plan before starting a discussion is usually a good idea, whether you've just run into a friend at the supermarket or a networking event.

The chat will have direction and won't seem awkward or uncomfortable if you have a clear objective.

If you see that the discussion is lagging, you may use the conversation's objective to bring up a new topic of discourse.

NVC WORKBOOK QUESTIONS FOR KIDS

Children need to learn how to comprehend and use NVC through these activities and their language. If you want to teach to different grades, they may be adjusted and customized as necessary.

Components of NVC Exercise:

1. Request that each student list the items they believed they needed but did not get. For example, "I didn't receive the kind of ice cream I wanted" or "My friend Henry wasn't here today for our class assignment, so now I have to do all the work while he stays at home" are basic examples of this.
2. After a short period of silence, ask each student to write an answer to one or two of those needs. For instance, you may reply, "Could I have strawberry ice cream instead," if someone said, "I didn't get the kind of ice cream I wanted."
3. Ask the kids to suggest a need they had that was unmet and the solution they came up with. Ask questions about their requirements and, if necessary, guide each kid who shares so that they may formulate an observation of the circumstances and their feelings.

Traversing the Components of NVC:

1. Ask each pupil to identify one individual whose behavior they don't like.

2. After each student has listed a person, ask them to list one activity that they dislike doing.

a. (This is the observation.)

3. Next, ask volunteers to read what they noted. Try to assist them in recreating their observations if they contain assessments. There are several ways to evaluate:

a. Blaming (She took my bus seat away from me. He gave me a nose punch.) Here's an illustration of how to turn them into observations: (On the bus, someone has taken my usual seat. I made fun of Paul, and he was upset.)

4. Assumptions (Sahra enjoys making fun of me. Joel believes I'm stupid.) Here's an illustration of how to turn things into observations: (Sarah called me "dumbo" because of my ears. "Kyle, you are stupid," Joel remarked.)

5. Judgment (He is cruel. She is not a reliable friend.) Here's an illustration of how to turn them into observations: (Alex steals my lunch money so he can buy himself ice cream. When I tell Katie a secret, she divulges it to everyone.)

6. Statements (He speaks excessively. They disregard the directions.) Here's an illustration of how to turn them into observations: (Whenever I try to talk about my day, he stops me with anecdotes. They keep playing on the swings even after I beg them to stop on the playground.)

After a few minutes, pick a handful of the observations above and instruct the students to work through the four NVC pillars one at a time.

Based on the observation, how do they feel as a result? (Feeling)

What needs—both theirs and the other person's—do they share? (Needs)

How could they tell the other person what they needed? (Requests)

(This request can be built up as I feel _____ Because I need/want. Could you please help me? Using the bus as an example, sitting in the seat that I like to be in would look like this:

"I'm angry because I want to sit here. Would you mind moving to another seat so I may take that place?

Exercise on Taking Ownership of Our Emotions:

1. Ask students to consider a time when they had a specific emotion, such as anger, sadness, or fear.

2. Next, instruct each pupil to write about the following different emotions:

   a. The circumstances surrounding the occurrence of the feeling
   b. What the specific feeling was that they experienced
   c. The cause of the emotion
   d. The origin of the emotion.

3. Request that everyone write out their potential responses to each of the four ways negative signals might be received once they have completed that assignment.

   a. Accusing ourselves
   b. Blaming other people
   c. Being aware of your wants and feelings
   d. Awareness of others' needs and feelings

6

CONFLICT RESOLUTION: GIVING AND RECEIVING AND APOLOGY

A fight occurs between two first-graders on the playground while they play kickball with other children. The one who accuses the other of cheating threatens to inform the teacher. The other youngster responds angrily, insisting he is not a cheater and never wants to play with him again. He walks with his head down away from the kickball field. Without him, the game continues.

It takes time to develop friendships, and there will always be hiccups. Although these ups and downs may seem small, broken friendships can result from unpleasant exchanges and friendships that change. For instance, the boy labeled a cheater decided to terminate the argument by leaving, but the issue wasn't truly settled.

The growth of healthy friendships depends on one's ability to resolve conflicts. For instance, a youngster who finds it difficult to manage their stress is likely to take their anger out on a buddy. When a disagreement arises, a youngster who struggles to resolve friendship issues could feel helpless. When there is disagreement, a youngster who lacks the language to express his emotions is prone to become paralyzed and shut down.

The good news is that young kids may learn how to handle difficult friendship circumstances by learning how to control their emotions and handle disagreements. Kids may learn to solve problems and keep their friendships intact even in the face of disagreement.

HATING IT WHEN YOU DON'T HAVE YOUR WAY

Every child has bad days. For a number of causes, children may exhibit less-than-ideal behaviors. They could be worn out, dissatisfied, or frustrated. They could be worn out following a particularly difficult day at school or have had too many sweets.

But what if the bad days become more common and the undesirable behaviors start to repeat themselves in a negative way?

A pattern of misbehavior or "acting out" may indicate that there is a larger issue at hand than just a poor day. Many people make the false assumption that persistent misbehavior simply necessitates stronger discipline. Instead, when kids act out, it may be a sign that something is wrong and they are unable to vocally communicate it.

Children do not naturally know how to communicate their emotions. Instead, they may act out their feelings by yelling, ignoring orders, or refusing to comply when situations get unpleasant, annoying, or frightening. Unwanted emotions can lead to a habit of troublesome, and occasionally harmful, actions if they are not acknowledged and dealt with.

What Is Acting Out?

The phrase "acting out" is frequently used to describe actions that parents find objectionable. The daily functioning of the family is disrupted by acting out behaviors. It's also normal for children to exhibit certain acting-out behaviors as they mature. Children may test the limits and defy parental control as they become more autonomous and develop their identities. By doing this, they may practice being independent in a secure setting. Children and teenagers may also act inappropriately to express difficult-to-express feelings, thoughts, or experiences.

Even while acting out is a common activity, each child's version of it is unique and depends on the child's personality, development, and coping mechanisms for stressful situations or unpleasant feelings. Nevertheless, every action, even a bad one, serves a purpose. Even if they are not conscious of what they desire, children act out to achieve a goal or satisfy a need.

For instance, a youngster who refuses to clean his room could be acting out. Then, his parents could neglect his tasks in order to focus on soothing him, thus escalating his outburst. The youngster discovers that throwing temper tantrums allows him to avoid doing things he dislikes, and he may act in this way to avoid other duties in the future.

Many inappropriate acts help kids satisfy their immediate needs. The issue arises when these actions continue to have an adverse influence on interpersonal relationships and daily functioning over time.

Common Reasons Children Act Out

Mental health specialists typically think kids act out at school or at home to accomplish a purpose. In his theory that individuals conduct in a certain manner to feel like they belong, psychiatrist and educator Rudolf Dreikurs outlined four purposes of misbehavior. Parents, teachers, and counselors are still led by Dreikurs' principles today. The following are his four misbehavior-related aims.

1. To Gain Attention

Children will take bad attention if they don't think a parent, teacher, or other authorized person is giving them the positive attention they desire. If no one else notices them, a youngster could feel unwelcome. As a result, a youngster who feels unappreciated would prefer to hear their parents rage at them. A youngster is likely acting out for attention if their conduct annoys a parent.

2. To Have Power

The places and circumstances that children find themselves in are often beyond their control. They have no control over whether they go to school or not and have no voice when a parent is away on a work trip. Children who act out have the opportunity to feel in charge when they would otherwise feel powerless.

A young toddler may use tantrums or defy parental orders to gain control. As the child ages, they could be even more motivated to control their destiny by engaging in negative activities or defying parental orders. When a child wants to be in charge, a parent could feel threatened and that they need to exert control over them.

3. To Get Revenge

Children may believe they are unwanted and only feel like they belong if they can make other people suffer through the same misery they are, so if they can't receive power or attention, they may seek a means to get even with one or both parents as a sort of punishment. Whatever it takes to punish them, they may utter cruel remarks or destroy a family member's property. Parents may get upset or astonished by their children's actions if they seek retribution.

4. To Display Inadequacy

Youngsters may act out if they feel they can't accomplish one of the objectives above or if they think they can't live up to their parents' expectations. Children who don't feel good enough may decline to engage in an activity or finish a task. They could avoid social settings and be reluctant to interact with people. The youngster is likely hiding behind the veil of inadequacy if a parent feels helpless and anxious to find a solution for their child.

IS CONFLICT THE END OF OUR FRIENDSHIP?

Do you and a buddy sometimes have a contentious argument? Do you fear that the conflict may destroy your friendship? What happens if you don't voice your worries?

It might be difficult to discover all of a sudden that you are at odds with a buddy. It's possible that you and your pal have been blissfully floating along for years then all of a sudden you find yourselves in this new territory. What's next? You actually have a lot of choices besides jumping ship. As you go through this new and strange stage, you will discover a lot about yourself, your companion, and your friendship.

Conflict is generally disturbing. It may be perplexing, depressing, and frightening. Each of us acquires a unique perspective on and approach to conflict as we mature. Parents, families, instructors, and schools teach us conflict resolution skills.

Conflict need not spell the end of your friendship. Instead of being a terrible thing or the end of a friendship, conflict may instead be a chance for transformation and progress in relationships, in every connection. In reality, settling a dispute amicably frequently leads to increased interpersonal harmony.

Some of us prefer to steer clear of disagreements in relationships. We could worry about the result. We can feel uneasy about what we anticipate transpiring. We could choose tooth extraction over the agony caused by fighting! Many individuals steer clear of conflict for many reasons.

The problem is that ignoring the disagreement will not make it go away. It does cause the problem to go unresolved, which might result in smoldering anger and a decline in friendship trust. However, we must, in a sense, choose our battles. Having arguments over every difference of opinion might not be beneficial to your friendship.

Here are some tips and approaches for resolving disagreements with friends:

- Respect for your friend, yourself, and your relationship is an important attitude to have while dealing with a disagreement. While discussing the issue, make a deliberate decision to treat everyone with respect.
- Listen closely and silently to your friend's thoughts, opinions, and concerns without responding.

- While preparing what you want to say or convey, use "I" statements and discuss the behavior or action causing you tension.
- Try to understand your friend's point of view. This might be quite challenging. especially if you have difficulty imagining your friend's point of view. These discrepancies can sometimes be disastrous. Can you accept each other's differing ideals or ideas while staying friends?
- Control your emotions while discussing your feelings. Can you ask for a break if you become hot around the collar and resume the conversation once you've cooled down?
- Determine which issues and values are important to each of you. Talk about your deal-breakers. Being aware of them, discussing them, talking about them, and communicating when there has been a breach might be the difference between a good and bad ending to a friendship.

HOW TO KNOW IF I'VE HURT MY FRIEND

A person's flaws and what irritates you about them may become more apparent the more you love them. Of course, if this person is your best friend, your connection with them will still be fantastic. Despite the occasional fights, you wouldn't exchange them for anything. You can get past some issues you would brood over with a casual companion.

However, even if you are familiar with them like the back of your hand, you could miss these indications that your closest buddy is upset with you.

Best friends are often very honest and strong enough to handle anything. Together, you've had some lows and, of course, some incredible highs. You truly root for and support each other to the finish because you love each other to the moon and back (and then some). But when you're at odds with your best buddy, it's incredibly difficult and challenging. And occasionally, even when you believe a problem has been handled, it may not be. Here are some techniques to formally end the conflict to determine whether your closest buddy is still upset with you.

There is some silence coming from their end.

Maybe you've said your bit and believe everything is done and good, but then you stop receiving their daily text. Now and again, they might send you memes or a status update about their lives, but lately, they've been relatively quiet. Yes, they reply to you, and everything is okay on the surface. To find out whether you all are okay, it could be worthwhile to delve further into what's going on.

There are one-worded responses.

They may sometimes be silent, but they can have very brief responses. Given that it will be so evident (particularly if you also do this when you're angry), this may not even be a hint you miss. It could not be anything; they might be busy or feel they don't need a longer response, which is reasonable. Once more, there is no harm in inquiring how things are.

They're kind of quiet in person.

Seeing how they behave in person if you frequently interact is worthwhile. It can be challenging to tell someone's mood or behavior from a text, particularly if you have a suspicion that they are upset with you. When there isn't one, your mind could give a text a negative attitude.

When you're hanging out, if your closest friend is likewise rather silent, it might be a red flag. Again, there are many more explanations for this. However, the chances are that this behavior isn't a coincidence if you believe they're still upset with you after a recent argument or if you did anything that could have irritated them.

WHAT TO DO IF MY FRIEND HURTS ME

Jake and Sam worked together. Moreover, they were close friends. After the current director departed, Sam intended to take over as department director, and Jake was aware that this was one of Sam's professional objectives. Jake had a different interest in the business. Sam thus believed he would have his friend's backing when the job became available. Rather, Jake told Sam, "Hey, bud. You have me to contend with for the director's job."

Sam was taken aback and said, "He's my best buddy. He knows I have been striving toward that job for a while. Never once did he show any interest in it. What's going on?"

Sam could talk to Jake about his feelings because they had been friends for so long. But his friend's response made him feel worse. Jake stated that if Sam was having problems, it was his fault since friends should be able to compete.

Jake's remark seems reasonable at first glance. Although it usually presents a considerably larger difficulty for female companions, competitiveness is a common component of men's friendships. For instance, men athletes frequently get along well with their toughest rivals, but female athletes appear to find this more difficult.

Sam believed Jake's actions were more motivated by backstabbing rather than competing: "If he were a close buddy, he would have talked to me before he went for the job. Otherwise, he wouldn't have pursued it at all."

Everyone has heard of the nasty middle school girls who seem to purposely harm their close pals simply for kicks. Bullies are a problem, as well. However, what should you do if a friend hurts you?

1. **Make sure you read the situation correctly.**
   Sometimes, our perceptions may not be accurate. It can just be our view, depending on our set of beliefs. For instance, a buddy of mine once felt that I had

betrayed him by breaking a commitment. I never pledged to it, though, in my mind. A disparity in perspective caused the miscommunication. We were able to bridge the divide between us after multiple conversations and attempts to rekindle our friendship.

2. **Try discussing the matter with your pal.** Since you can't reality-test your views without your friend's input, this is related to the first stage. This type of conversation usually results in a solution. However, there are situations when the outcome isn't what you want or expect like it was with Jake and Sam.
3. **Talk about it with another person you trust.** If you can't persuade your friend to open up to you, discuss the situation with someone whose opinion you appreciate. However, avoid engaging in gossip. Turning a shared friend against a buddy who has harmed you may seem nice at the moment, but it will only make things worse. It's not the same as criticizing a buddy behind their back to receive counsel from a neutral, disinterested party.
4. **Seek means to resolve the dispute.** Occasionally, this is only just waiting until you both have cooled off. According to Daniel Goleman, the author of several books about emotional intelligence, we all need time to calm off to manage conflict. You may give your body and mind an opportunity to reset by taking a break, engaging in physical activity, or

even getting a full night's sleep so that you don't keep having the same debates and coming to a deadlock.

5. **Let it go.** Find a method to let go of your pain, bitterness, and grief, whether you prevail in the argument or not, or decide to remain friends. Sometimes we have to consciously choose to let go and move on, and this takes time. You don't do yourself or your friendships any favors by holding onto hurt and anguish. The best thing you can do after a disagreement is to reflect on what you've learned so you can put it to use the next time.
6. **Don't generalize about all of your buddies.** There are occasions when those we believe to be on our side turn out to be against us. If this occurs, don't seek retribution; instead, get over the hurt and move on. Various buddies can assist with this.

Sam eventually received the job but also lost his friend. "I didn't trust him anymore," Jake said because he felt betrayed.

HOW TO APOLOGIZE AND MEAN IT

It might be frightening and nerve-wracking to admit you made a mistake and then apologize to someone. Here are some suggestions that could help.

This might be helpful if you need to apologize to someone you don't know, want to explain yourself effectively in a challenging circumstance, or struggle to get things off your chest.

Why It's Difficult to Apologize

Even excellent people have terrible days sometimes. Unfortunately, your mind has to work extra hard to convince you that you're the one in the wrong when you have to own up to acting like a jerk. That wasn't a fun experience.

We struggle to apologize because we don't want to make ourselves feel bad. Since we work so hard to maintain a positive self-image, it can be challenging to apologize sincerely.

Why It's Crucial to Admit Our Mistakes

Every part of our lives, including the job, school, and relationships, can suffer from our inability to own up to our errors and honestly apologize to someone when we need to. It may also stop us from developing and learning lessons from our experiences.

How to Apologize

It's crucial to begin by speaking a few encouraging words to yourself. This is referred to as "self-affirmation" and improves how you view yourself. It has been demonstrated that self-affirmation lowers tension and anxiety while boosting self-esteem and confidence.

Consider your core beliefs and best traits, such as your skills and interests, accomplishments at work or in school, or how you treat your loved ones and friends. You may tell yourself, "I'm amazing at coming up with new ideas," or "I'm kind to everyone I meet," for instance.

1. **Before you apologize to someone, using self-affirmation can make your apology more honest and authentic.** You may lower your guard by telling yourself, "Hey, there are so many excellent things about you; one mistake doesn't change anything," and you'll feel better.
2. **Explain your desire to apologize.** Although it may seem simple, the first step in apologizing is to describe your actions in detail before expressing regret. It demonstrates to the other person that you are aware of your error. Before you apologize, practicing your speech in detail can be a good idea. Say, "I snapped at you yesterday," for instance.
3. **Admit you were wrong.** It's critical to demonstrate to the other person your willingness to accept responsibility for your actions and confess that you made a mistake. Saying, "It was wrong of me to talk to you in the way I did," is an example.
4. **Acknowledge the other person's feelings.** A proper apology requires demonstrating that you are aware of the effects of your actions on the other person. This shows them that you are aware of their suffering. Say something like, "I realize you must

have been incredibly unhappy, furious, and bewildered."

5. **Express regret.** A simple "I'm sorry" will demonstrate your sincerity. Don't add a "but" at the end of that phrase; keep it short.
6. **Request their forgiveness.** Saying, "I realize it will take time, but I sincerely hope we can still be friends" or "Is there anything I can do to make things right" will help you ask for forgiveness. This communicates to the other person how significant their connection is to you.

Show that you're sorry.

It's crucial to express your sorrow for what you did by doing so, not simply by saying it. Consider how you can correct the situation and repair the issue, if feasible. For instance, you may assist a friend by replacing the item if you misplaced or damaged something that belonged to someone else.

However, certain situations cannot be resolved, such as when you have offended a buddy. The best action in this situation is to prevent it from happening again and demonstrate your real remorse via your actions. To demonstrate that you're taking action to ensure it doesn't happen again, you might also indicate that you've identified an issue you can address.

For instance, you may remark, "I see that I have trouble regulating my anger, and snapping at others is unfair." I'm attempting to pay closer attention to when this occurs.

It takes a lot of guts to accept responsibility for your actions and extend an apology. At first, it will be unsettling, but mastering this genuine skill over time may greatly enhance your interactions with others around you. You can do this.

WORKBOOK QUESTIONS ON FORGIVENESS FOR KIDS

Do I want to be forgiving?

....

Why is it necessary to forgive?

....

Why should I forgive someone who has wronged me?

....

What makes forgiving so crucial?

....

When you forgive, are you doing yourself a favor?

....

Why should you forgive rather than harbor resentment?

....

Why is forgiving difficult?

....

What is the health impact of forgiveness?

....

7

MAKING AND KEEPING GREAT FRIENDS

For the majority of youngsters, attending birthday parties, playing with other kids, and having a best friend are common activities.

Friendships aid in a child's emotional and moral growth and social development. Children not only learn how to interact with others, but strong friendships may also play a crucial role in teaching them how to regulate their emotions and express them in healthy ways. However, some kids experience social difficulties and have difficulty developing and maintaining friendships.

It might be upsetting for both of you if your child doesn't seem to have friends or is seldom (or never) invited to play with other kids. Many kids might want extra help interacting with their classmates. You may support children in establishing strong connections and navigating their social environment in various ways.

WHAT MAKES FRIENDSHIPS IMPORTANT?

A child's social and emotional development depends heavily on making friends as they grow up. Children who have friends are more confident and self-assured. Positive relationships can act as a barrier against bullying.

According to some studies, youngsters with strong connections may be better able to deal with bullying when it does occur and assist bullies to stay away (Navarro et al., 2018.)

Healthy relationships can impart valuable life lessons, such as working together with others.

Children that have strong connections gain dispute resolution skills and social skills. Children who have strong connections feel more empowered because they feel identity and belonging. Peer pressure is advantageous in these circumstances, particularly if children support one another in fostering an interest in community service and social justice.

Additionally, friendships matter at practically every age. Even though group play doesn't completely develop until children are three, toddlers tend to play with pals and play together. Therefore, it's never too early to support your youngster in learning how to form friendships.

If you are unsure whether your child has friends, speak with their instructors to learn more about how they get along with other students at school. To better understand how successfully they're forming connections, you may also question your child about their friendships.

Additionally, if they are happy with the number of friends they currently have, they should refrain from making the idea of making friends a greater deal than it has to be. Keep in mind that while some kids seem to have many friends, others only need a select group of close pals.

WHO ARE GOOD FRIENDS?

How many friends do you have? No need to keep score! Just consider it for a moment. Most likely, you have more friends than you think. Your school has buddies. You have neighbors who are pals. Most likely, you would refer to your family as your friends. You may even be friends with people from your church and sports teams!

How many of your pals would you say are good friends? People occasionally use the term "good" "to express that a person is a close friend. However, we are discussing the term "good" to symbolize a quality friend or the complete opposite of a terrible friend.

You've undoubtedly heard from your parents and instructors how important it is to have close friends as you age. Having excellent friends around you makes life more joyful and full. But what qualities distinguish a good friend?

Although everyone has a different idea of what makes a good friend, most people would agree on some features, attributes, and characteristics that define a good friend. Let's examine a few characteristics of "excellent" friends."

When you ask people what makes a good friend, you frequently receive responses that can be summed up in one word: presence. When you need them, a good friend will be there. Good friends are there for you in good times and bad, whether supporting you through the pain of losing a loved one or being by your side while you're ill.

You don't have to be going through the trouble to appreciate a wonderful buddy. Being there for a buddy might sometimes mean listening when they need to chat, helping with homework, or even helping to look for a lost phone.

Action is one of the cornerstones of being there for a friend. Despite what people say, deeds always speak louder than words, as the proverb says." A good friend will truly be there to help when troubles emerge, unlike someone who may promise to be there for you when you need them.

Loyalty is a key characteristic of a good buddy. Everybody has moments when they aren't the most pleasant person to be around. Maybe we messed up, or we're just in a lousy mood. True friends accept you for who you are in good and terrible times.

In addition to being honest, true friends will let you know when you aren't a good friend to them. Some people want to be among people who will give them the information they want to hear. Even if you don't want to hear it, good friends will tell you what you need to hear.

Most people desire trustworthy buddies in addition to great friends who are reliable, honest, and present. It might be difficult to think of someone Who are good friends? Ask a good friend if you can't depend on them. A strong friendship that might last a lifetime is built on mutual trust between friends.

Communication is just another of those dependable foundational elements of enduring friendships. Do you have a friend that always completes your sentences for you? You two could be so closely aligned that you don't even need to exchange words to seem to know what the other is thinking. That intense connection is rare and unmistakably indicative of a wonderful buddy.

We could talk about a lot more characteristics of wonderful buddies. Some people place greater value on some traits than others. Everybody needs to define their standards for what it means to be a good friend. And it implies that in your relationships with your friends, you must also exhibit those traits.

Find people who will let you be who you are and not someone else, and be who you are. Respect each other's boundaries and encourage one another. Always look for the best in people and treat them with respect. Never assume that the wonderful buddy you make today won't become a lifelong companion!

HOW TO MAKE GOOD FRIENDS

Although friendship is a vital aspect of life, not all kids are naturally good at it, and that's okay. You may learn how to make and maintain friends. Your youngster will soon have a friend or two they can hang out with with a little work, courage, and time.

Find out how your youngster feels about making friends. On the first day of school, they could be anxious about making small talk with children on the playground or sitting at a new lunch table. Perhaps they would like to approach the other children but are unsure how they will be treated.

After determining if your kid is content or trapped, you can construct a strategy to assist them in acquiring the social skills they need to make wholesome friends.

Build Conversation Skills

Your youngster may need to practice starting and keeping up discussions with others and taking turns while speaking and asking questions about other people. Provide your child with conversation starters like "What do you do for fun?" and "Do you have any pets?" until they can intuitively pick up on other people's cues.

You may also use TV shows as examples of how individuals converse with one another. Mentioning body language, tone of voice, and conversational pauses are crucial indications while conversing with people. Role-playing interactions might assist them in getting the necessary practice.

Practice Listening

Strong social abilities and understanding of how to express interest in others are key components of being a good friend. Because of this, you might want to concentrate on helping your child develop their capacity for empathy and listening.

Healthy displays of empathy and care for others can lead to new friendships. Ask your child to think of ways they may be kind to children their age.

Discuss with your youngster how to identify when someone is going through a difficult period. Teach them how to be kinder. Your youngster may, for instance, bake cookies for a friend whose animal is ill or mail a sympathy note to a person who has lost a loved one. An excellent technique to demonstrate empathy to a possible new buddy is to take the time to let them know you care.

Look for Opportunities to Interact with Peers

Your youngster may lack friends simply because they haven't had enough opportunities to make them. Finding friends might be easier if you participate in plenty of activities with kids your age who share your interests. Giving your youngster more chances to connect with other kids might be beneficial.

Find methods to include your child in extracurricular activities or at school. Naturally, pay attention to both your child's temperament and activity level. Children that are introverted and require time alone to recharge shouldn't have a full schedule.

Where to Look for Opportunities for Friendship

Whatever activity your child loves, there will undoubtedly be chances for them to meet others along the road. Start by assisting kids in determining what they enjoy or find fascinating.

The demand for children to interact with others is lessened when they participate in organizations or activities that excite or interest them. In addition to doing something they like, they are also in the company of others who share their feelings. And discussions regarding what they are doing or experiencing might frequently come up.

It would help if you also urged your children to seek out friends who are different from themselves. Kids may learn so much from someone with whom they do not think they share much in common.

You can make some recommendations to see if anything sounds interesting if your youngster has trouble coming up with ideas for what they enjoy and dislike.

You might try:

- Tennis, martial arts, swimming, or jogging clubs are individual sports.
- Non-competitive activities like painting and music classes, robotics classes, or chess clubs
- Other clubs, such as religious youth groups, 4-H, and scouting organizations
- Book clubs or storytimes at your local library or bookshop
- The playground, park, swimming pool, trampoline park, or other common play locations
- Opportunities for community service where they may assist other children, such as a local food bank or a clean-up program.
- Team sports for children, such as soccer, baseball, basketball, and volleyball

If you're worried that your youngster may be anxious about meeting new people, bring an icebreaker with you, like a toy, a pet, or some snacks, to gently introduce your kid to other kids. This is especially useful if your child isn't extroverted by nature.

CONVERSATION SKILLS TO NURTURE YOUR FRIENDSHIP

Questioning

The subject that people enjoy discussing the most is themselves. The benefit of asking questions to create friends is not surprising.

Step 1: Find out what topics individuals like discussing the most. When we asked our sons about their "hobbies," they cited a few particular video games and hit movies at the time.

Step 2: Share that individuals love to talk about themselves

Step 3: Come up with a list of inquiries you can make of individuals. Make some notes.

Step 4: is to role-play a conversation while alternately asking and responding to questions.

Step 5: Have them practice on a student and let you know how it goes. Remind them to ask questions whenever they get the chance to interact with other children.

Sharing

People might be drawn to us or turned away depending on how we reveal information about ourselves.

Step 1: Ask, "Consider someone you love. How do they phrase it when they talk about themselves? Talk about several ways individuals can communicate information about themselves and the words and phrases that spring to mind, such as "know-it-all," "proud," and "modest."

Step 2: What do you like to share about yourself? Talk about their interests, hobbies, and other things they're proud of and like discussing with their pals.

Step 3: Come up with ideas for knowledge sharing that don't seem arrogant or conceited. Talk about your voice tone and your choice of words.

Step 4: Continue your practice! Also, please encourage them to balance talks by asking and sharing during the first communication skill, so they aren't always talking about themselves.

Extending Invitations

This type of invitation-extending does not apply to your child's yearly birthday celebration. We have the chance to invite additional folks daily. The question "Would you want to sit with me at lunch today?" is a common invitation for children. and "Would you want to play basketball during the break?"

Step 1: Identify several activities kids have encouraged you to participate in that make you feel included.

Step 2: Make a list of several invites that your child may issue to other children.

Step 3: Pretend to issue a casual invitation that sounds welcoming and not overly formal. Include advice on how to behave politely when someone rejects. Additionally, teach your youngster that it's OK for someone to turn down an invitation. Although it's vital to be aware that children may, for various reasons, not feel like participating or doing what your child is inviting them to, it's crucial to know that children with social skills deficiencies frequently perceive the rejection of an invitation as "bullying." Try to explain what this means.

Step 4: Have them practice their invitation skills in the real world and come back to you with an update on how they fared and whether they were interacting more with other children.

8

PRACTICAL EXERCISES AND ACTIVITIES GUIDE

This section will help kids practice their knowledge of what social skills mean. It also includes activities for parents to do with their children in order to help them socialize better.

ACTIVITIES YOU CAN DO ON YOUR OWN

Role Playing

The value of role-playing can be emphasized as a successful method for kids to make sense of their surroundings.

Simple Role Play Ideas for Kids

1. Hospital

One of the most popular role-playing scenarios is a nurse seeing a patient, a doctor consulting in their office, or a hospital surgery. Give the team some white jackets and medical supplies to use. What can you use to check your blood pressure or as an x-ray machine?

2. Baking and Cooking

Many toddlers and preschoolers engage in this hobby, often for years at a time. Kids naturally like pretending to make food (sometimes invisible) and bring it to you since eating is a significant aspect of everyday life, and they witness their parents do it every day. Raid your kitchen to get the necessary props; it's also simple to make substitutions. In a kitchen, a wooden block may be many different things.

3. Restaurant

Kids who play "restaurant" like the entire set-up, including the tablecloth, fake menus, a waiter in an apron, pen and paper for taking orders, etc., more than simply the cooking. Children take turns playing the roles of the waiter and the customer while eating fake food (if you'd prefer to use actual food, use these culinary activities). Recall making the subsequent meal payment!

4. Shop

Another favorite among children is playing store. You may either keep it straightforward or go creative with this. Set up a grocery store sign, shelves, items for sale, price tags, shopping baskets, a cash register, and even some pretend money. Making store props is a great approach to including creative art in various ways. What type of store are your children opening? Is it a market, a garment, or a gift shop?

5. Mother and father

When they are still toddlers, young children frequently begin acting like they are taking care of newborns. Since taking care of others was their first experience, they naturally like playing this position. They like playing the role of parents, feeding, putting to sleep, changing, and comforting their infant. To perform this role, children can use dolls and personal belongings from when they were babies. They also like strolling infants in actual or toy strollers.

ACTIVITIES TO DO WITH THE HELP OF YOUR PARENT/GUARDIAN

Playing Host to Other Kids in Your House

Organizing a Teen Party

Your youngster might occasionally wish to arrange a party at home. It might be stressful to host a party because you could be concerned about loud music, gatecrashing, property damage, or alcohol consumption.

But with the correct preparation, throwing a party for your child can be thrilling and entertaining. Your kid will be able to practice planning, grow in responsibility, and gain decision-making skills. A party is a great opportunity for you to meet your child's pals.

Parties frequently and significantly influence teenage social life. Talking to your child about balancing enjoyment and safety is a good idea if they want to attend a party.

Organizing Playdates

Take your kids to play with pals as often as possible by inviting friends over for a playdate. Sibling play is another beneficial kind of engagement.

Your youngster will practice socializing more if they have more chances to interact with others.

If your small child is not yet at ease being alone with a buddy, do not let them. Allow them time to earn their trust.

OTHERS: 150+ PRACTICAL EXERCISES AND ACTIVITIES TO IMPROVE SOCIAL INTELLIGENCE IN CHILDREN AND TEENAGERS

1. Theater

Getting involved in theater is a terrific way for kids to meet new people and broaden their perspectives. Find out if there are any openings for children by visiting the local theater companies in your town or city. In a creative setting, a theater may encourage your gregarious child to flourish and encourage your shy child to open out. Children who prefer to stay out of the spotlight can think about working in theater organizations' production or costume departments. Additionally, you ought to urge your kid to participate in school performances.

2. Activity Camps

Kids of all ages will love summer camps with many exciting activities. Locate a camp that is suitable for your teen. Camps are fantastic locations to meet new people, engage in conversation, and collaborate with them. Teens who lack social skills benefit most from the day or overnight programs. Even timid children can gain the skills necessary for appropriate social interactions after spending the day engaging with new people and participating in various activities. There are numerous alternatives for camps, including those in science, sports, dance, theatre, and other genres.

3. Volunteering

Kids of all ages can benefit from volunteering. Your teen should be encouraged to volunteer in nursing homes, child welfare organizations, or animal shelters. They can offer to read books to younger children or teach them essential skills. Please help them to comprehend how to plan volunteer activities that benefit their area or community. Your teen can serve others and develop his social skills at the same time.

4. Participation in Sports

There is a reason why sports are so important in life. Sports may teach individuals a lot more than just fun. Sports may teach teenagers the importance of cooperation, planning, leadership, inspiration, fitness, and support. All of these traits are excellent for enhancing socializing abilities and character development.

5. Art Classes

By encouraging your teen's artistic talent, you can also help them develop social skills. Your teen will have the opportunity to express himself creatively while also interacting with teachers and other pupils. The activity improves the communication skills of timid children. Encourage your teenagers to sign up for any art or craft classes simply to try it out. Teenagers can better communicate with others when participating in activities like painting workshops, sketching, fabric art, pottery making, and sculpting.

6. Bonfire Night

Plan nights around bonfires for your teen. Plan gatherings so your extended family can attend, and you can all reconnect or remember earlier times. Encourage your teenagers to host a unique birthday celebration with a bonfire night as the ideal setting for a fun night with friends.

7. Educational Trips

Isn't it great that your teen enjoys visiting museums? Organize activities that will help them develop their social skills. Visit many nearby towns and all the museums. By taking your teens to bookstores where they can purchase historical books, you can encourage them to pursue their passion further. Discover relevant expert talks and seminars, and either offer to go with them or pay for your teen to attend with a buddy.

8. Game Nights

A great way to encourage teenagers to interact with others at a party or family function is to have game night. Ask participants to develop games on the spot to make such exercises more exciting. Have a great time and vote for the best ones. The bonding will aid in your teen's socialization skills improvement.

9. Live Events

Taking your teen to see live events with family or friends can be a memorable experience. Teenagers can attend events such as championship games, dancing performances, music recitals, quiz shows, tournaments, etc., in a social setting. A large group of strangers would surround them in the crowd. Your teen will be able to let go of his inhibitions while supporting his favorite team.

10. Bowling Fun

Arrange an evening of fun with your teen, including bowling, roller skating, or ice skating. Being around many people on such visits might be great for your teen's social skills development. He will be able to shatter his bubble when he bowls or skates in front of onlookers.

11. Eye on the Forehead

Put a sticker of an eye or a pair of eyes on your forehead when you are with your kid. Motivate them to examine the stickers. Even though it might not be looking directly into your eyes, it teaches them to look in the appropriate place in a comical, less scary manner.

12. Build The Vocab

You will require: cooking equipment, a toy, and stationary

How to play: Give your youngster a piece of equipment and ask him to explain it from his point of view. She needs to transform the object into something it is not. He sees an empty cup as anything from a party hat to a duck's bill.

Children participating in this social skill training will improve their vocabulary and narrative abilities.

13. Setting The Table

You'll require markers, scissors, two-sided tape, and seven different colored construction paper hues.

How to play: Set the table so your young child can watch and learn.

Please have your child cut out the following from the construction paper after drawing it.

- Dinner knife
- Serving fork
- Water bottle
- Napkin

14. Soft Or Loud?

Another simple game to improve your child's listening abilities is provided here. They must concentrate and distinguish between loud and soft sounds, which is useful when you ask them to use "quiet voices" in the future.

Start by creating mild or loud noises with various objects, such as two blocks being loudly slammed together. Then inquire as to whether the noise was loud or soft.

15. Space Invader

Required: Sticks from popsicles, cartoon aliens, crayons, glue

How to play: Instruct your child to color the alien cartoon pictures. Allow him to cut it out now.

Attach the images of the alien on the popsicle sticks. Explain to your child the significance of respecting others' space as you attach the images. You can also teach him the idea of using "soft hands" rather than hitting or yelling to grab someone's attention.

Tell him you are the invader, while the aliens he has colored are you.

The aliens need time to gather after the child displays his space invader mark. Make him follow suit.

You can explain to him the idea of allowing individuals their place to play in this way.

16. A Single-Question Interview

Required: Cards and a pen

How to play: Write straightforward inquiries like "Do you have a pet?" and "What is your favorite food?" on the cards.

Children should sit in a circle. Distribute the cards and instruct each person to read the question aloud.

Give the children five minutes to split up into pairs in another room.

Instruct the children to exchange questions and listen to each other's responses.

Next, ask each child directly what they discovered about the relationship.

The game will teach the kids about one another and promote active listening.

17. Telephone Skills

A preschool activity that teaches kids social skills over the phone

Required: numbers on round stickers, cardboard-style paper, miniature sticky notes, scissors

How to play: Tell your youngster to use the card stock paper to create a model of a phone. Cut a rectangle out of card stock, and then use round number stickers to create a duplicate of the phone's keyboard.

Now give your child your number and the number of your partner, and instruct him to practice dialing and making calls. You can also instruct him on how to call 911.

As soon as your child phones your number, start speaking to him on your phone. Just as you would with any other adult, conduct a dialogue. In this manner, you can instruct your child in phone manners and communication techniques.

18. Improvisational Storytelling

Some kids may have delayed social skills, especially those with specific needs. One such social skills exercise for autistic people is this.

You'll need images depicting emotions.

How to play: Lay the emotional imagery down on the surface, face down.

Now instruct the players to consider the essential components of the story. Anything could be from a lemur to a dog to a banana.

Requesting that the first player select a card and begin his tale. He is free to go on whatever path he wants with the narrative. But there's a catch—he has to express the feeling on his card.

After he is finished, allow another child to choose a card and make up a narrative. Children must build on one another's ideas while incorporating all the narrative components.

19. Swinging

Maintain eye contact with your child while they swing. Make it into a game where the kid must use their feet to try to get to you. The sensory stimulation could be relaxing and help them concentrate better on you.

20. "Freeze It"

How to play: Gather the children in the hallway or yard.

Ask the other kids to line horizontally and choose an "it."

Ask the children to now become immobile statues. The "it" must now make an effort to amuse the other participants.

The child who laughs first will be the "it" for the following round.

Children will learn self-control and patience through the game, two important social qualities.

21. Etiquette and More

Middle school pupils benefit personally from social skills training exercises. This is an example of a social skill-building activity for kids that can aid their understanding and subsequent growth.

Requirements: Construction paper, magazine, glue, scissors, markers, crayons

Talk to your children about appropriate and inappropriate behavior first. Tell them that the distinction between excellent and terrible manners isn't very wide. Consider the difference between standing up to greet an elder person and sitting down.

Now instruct them to use the magazine cutouts to create a collage on proper and impolite behavior. You might even request that they create a motto emphasizing etiquette.

22. Word Strips

Requirements: Paper, pens, and double-sided tape

Draw and cut out words like "peace," "clean," "quiet," "neat," and "hygiene."

Now discuss the pertinent regulations with him, such as "keeping the clothing neat," "remaining silent when someone is on the phone," and so forth.

Now, cut off the strips and instruct your youngster to adhere to them as he sees fit.

23. What Sound?

Watching kids make different sounds with this one may be very entertaining. Children should first sit back to back. Ask the other person to guess each time one makes a sound (maybe an animal sound). Then switch.

24. Staring Competition

Many kids find it difficult to maintain eye contact during a conversation. A staring competition can help kids establish and maintain eye contact so they can concentrate on that job rather than trying to talk at the same time.

You might start more gently if your child is still uneasy. Put a sticker on your forehead for them to see, then start a discussion afterward.

25. Roll the Ball

It's never too early to begin developing social skills, and toddlers can enjoy a game of roll the ball. Kids build the groundwork for other social skills by passing a ball back and forth in turns.

Children acquire the ability to take turns in conversation and during group activities. They practice self-control by rolling the ball with just enough force to reach their friend but not too much.

26. Virtual Playtime

When in-person play dates are not possible, your child can still interact with friends via video chat and other online platforms. Kids participating in video chats can practice eye contact by gazing at their virtual acquaintances.

When it comes to their future workplace, the ability to learn to adjust to new circumstances becomes an important skill. Creating new activities to do together improves problem-solving skills, adding to essential social skills.

27. Staring Contest

Many kids find it difficult to maintain eye contact during a conversation. A staring competition can help kids establish and maintain eye contact so they can concentrate on that job rather than trying to talk at the same time.

You might start more gently if your child is still uneasy. Put a sticker on your forehead for them to see, then start a discussion afterward.

28. Roll the Ball

It is never too early to start developing social skills, and toddlers can have fun playing roll the ball. Kids build the groundwork for other social skills by passing a ball back and forth in turns.

Children acquire the ability to take turns in conversation and during group activities. They practice self-control by rolling the ball with just enough force to reach their friend but not too much.

29. "Mother, May I?"

Another childhood classic that calls for conformity.

The "mother" is one child facing the line of kids from a distance.

Then "Mother" picks one child at a time and directs them. These instructions follow a formula, like "Luke may take three gigantic strides ahead" or "Hannah, you may take four baby steps forward."

When the youngster asks, "Mother, may I?," the mother either says "yes" or "no." The conversation must start over if the youngster forgets to respond, "Mother, may I?"

Whoever gets to "mother" first wins.

30. Emotion Charades

Writing various emotions on paper strips is part of the emotion charades game. Your youngster chooses one from a hat or bucket. Then, they need to try acting that feeling out.

Children can learn to identify emotions using body language and facial signals by playing emotion charades. Even better, you can modify these social skills-building exercises to turn them into an emotional-drawing Pictionary-style game for kids.

Children learn emotion management, crucial for fostering strong connections and effectively communicating sentiments, by describing and acting out emotional expressions and reactions in social skills exercises.

31. Expression Mimicking Games

You can teach social skills to your child by playing this game with them. Your toddler can learn the meaning of many expressions by imitating your facial expressions, which helps them identify them when others use them in natural conversation.

Children with social difficulties feel more at ease around people when they can understand facial expressions.

32. Topic Game

The topic game has several variations, but the most popular one involves picking a topic and giving each letter of the alphabet a name for anything that belongs in that category. If you decide to write about animals, for instance, you might write:

- Dwarf aardvark
- Baboon.
- Chicken

Kids learn to focus on one topic and follow instructions by playing the topic game until the task is finished. They are also able to connect disparate letters and think of unique solutions.

33. Step into Conversation

For kids with autism, there is a card game called Step Into Conversation. The game offers planned social skills exercises, including striking up conversations and discussing particular card-based topics.

The game teaches young players how to converse politely with others and to do so while maintaining perspective and empathy. Demonstrating how to respectfully initiate a conversation, when to talk, and when to listen teaches excellent manners and self-control.

You can give talks structure and help children develop the social skills they need to deal with many circumstances in daily life by using socialization games like this one.

34. "Please And Thank" You Game

Playing this game before a formal dinner, such as Christmas or Thanksgiving, is a fun way to learn good table manners. To pass, make up fake platters of food. On the plates, have the children create images of different foods like pie, mashed potatoes, and turkey. The images are then adhered to paper plates to be passed. Additionally, you might print them from the internet or cut them out of publications.

How to play:

- First "dish" should be addressed.
- Ask the kid to identify the meal.
- Ask them if they enjoy it.
- Ask them to say "No, thank you" if they don't like it.
- "Please, yes," if they do.
- Following that, they ask the following child, "Would you like some_____?
- The youngster can then say "No, thank you" or "Yes, please" in response.
- Continue until all of the "dishes" have been passed.

35. Game of Names

In this straightforward game, kids yell out a person's name and then roll or toss a ball to that person. Even young children might benefit from social skills exercises like this to help them remember the names of their peers. It demonstrates their receptivity to others and represents a step toward getting to know others.

36. Simon Says

Children learn impulse control, self-discipline, and listening skills through Simon Says as they mimic their classmates' actions and directions. Additionally, it encourages good behavior and awards players who adhere to the rules throughout the game.

37. Rhythm Games

Both at home and in the classroom, rhythm games can be used as a social skills activity. These musical activities encourage your child's creativity while teaching them to follow instructions and spot patterns.

Kirschner and Tomasello's 2010 study demonstrates how making music together improves social behavior. The researchers discovered that in a game where youngsters had to "wake the frogs" with music, those who played by the rules were more willing to assist those who sought to wake the frogs without music.

38. Playing with Characters

These social skills activities encourage play by using your child's innate need to play. You can communicate with your child through the toys by interacting with dolls or plush animals.

By talking to their toys, kids learn to understand how other people act and how to show how they feel. They can play pretend with the toys and work on their social skills without worrying about upsetting the toys.

39. Play Pretend

Typically, children will conjure up a situation in which they pretend to be someone or something else. They might pretend to be parents, play house, or pretend to be a doctor, a veterinarian, a teacher, or a cashier. These circumstances give children the chance to experiment with various social skills exercises.

For instance, as they act out the role of a parent to another child, they must develop their capacity to identify emotions, manage conflict, and adjust to changing circumstances.

40. Token Stack

Token stacks from board games like checkers can be modified to make social skills exercises that teach kids how to converse politely. A token is added to the child's stack each time they talk and reply appropriately.

While taking turns speaking, they must attempt to stack their tokens as high as possible. Due to this exercise, they concentrate on maintaining a relaxed discussion and providing intelligent answers to queries and assertions.

41. Decision-Making Games

There are numerous ways to engage in social skills exercises like decision-making games. Your youngster can learn persistence, consideration, and teamwork through strategy games or basic sorting and matching exercises.

These games assist children who struggle with indecision by encouraging them to choose even if it isn't the best option initially. If they make a mistake, it encourages them to try again by illustrating low-risk repercussions.

42. Building Game

Children must communicate, take turns, and understand one another when building something with one another, like a tower out of blocks.

Children will brainstorm ways to construct their objects in groups. When kids use it, they discover how to try again if the invention fails and to recognize one other's special talents when they complete the task successfully.

43. Participatory Gardening

In contrast to other social skills exercises, community gardening teaches kids how to care for a live object.

Having your child take care of something helps them learn responsibility since they can't just leave their plants to die. Gardening with other people helps them learn how to get along with others. In addition to getting youngsters outside, this exercise can also relax them.

44. Team Sports

Children can play on a recreational team, at school, or even with their pals in the backyard. Team sports teach children how to cooperate for a common cause while maintaining their attention on the game.

They also learn how to react appropriately when they win or lose and recognize emotions, such as when someone is hurt or scores a goal.

45. Productive Debate

A fruitful debate works well for older children to learn how to control their emotions and practice using positive expression even under trying circumstances. They get the ability to handle challenging conversations without becoming angry or trying to belittle the other person.

Debate and listening skills help people gain stronger leadership qualities essential for classroom and business success.

46. Scavenger Hunts

Children collaborate to collect items or earn a prize after scavenger hunts. Students develop collaboration, organization, and good decision-making skills as they work toward their objectives. They might decide to cooperate, move as a team, or break up to get to the game's conclusion.

Additionally, they are rewarded for complying. By creating puzzles for other players to solve, these activities boost their capacity for creative problem-solving.

47. Turn-Taking Games

Babies and young children are capable of spontaneous deeds of compassion, although they can be wary of strangers. So how do we impart the concept of a buddy to them?

One effective technique is to have the youngster perform reciprocal, lighthearted acts of kindness with the stranger. For instance, the youngster can roll a ball back and forth or alternately push a toy's button. The youngster and the stranger can exchange intriguing objects.

48. Broken Telephone

The greatest place to play the silent game Broken Telephone is inside. These are the guidelines:

The first step is to circle up.

One person speaks and whispers something to the person sitting next to them.

After then, the message is passed on to the following individual.

She speaks the phrase aloud once it has reached the final participant in the circle.

Sending the message intact around the circle is the object of the game.

You can improve your hearing abilities by playing this game. Your child may benefit from engaging in social interactions and developing social skills with peers. As they attempt to hear what the speaker is whispering, kids also develop their ability to recognize sounds.

It is also a ton of fun because the message frequently gets "broken" on the road and makes kids laugh out loud!

49. Story Time Clap

Clapping is a fantastic peaceful game to enjoy with your toddlers. Decide whether to read a book or tell a story. The kids must clap whenever they hear a specific word or phrase throughout the story.

50. Touch-and-Feel Box

For your youngsters, a touch-and-feel box is yet another entertaining pastime. Start by gathering some objects with distinctive textures. Then, place them in an opaque box or bag to the naked eye.

Everyone in the room should silently touch and feel one of the objects as you go around the room. Have them disclose what they believe is in the bag after everyone has taken a chance.

Check to see how many kids successfully identified an object.

A fantastic technique to develop their language is with the Touch and Feel Box. To express their feelings, people must link their sensations with language.

51. "I Spy"

I Spy can be played inside or outside. These are the guidelines:

One participant selects an item from the space.

Then they remark, "I spy with my little eye, something," and then they name the color they saw.

Everyone else in the group makes educated guesses as to what that thing might be.

The only options are yes or no.

This game promotes both social interaction and critical thinking. It encourages conversation among the kids and helps them grow as social beings. They must also listen to learn the color and what other people are speculating.

52. Musical Chairs

Children can learn to let go and have fun with other kids by playing with musical chairs.

Chairs should first be arranged in a circle. There needs to be one fewer chair where kids are playing.

Everyone moves around the chairs as soon as the music starts. Everyone must locate a chair to sit on when the music ends. The game is over for the player without a chair. Take away one more chair after each round.

Up until there is just one chair left, the game goes on. Whoever occupies the final seat wins!

Your kids will learn excellent listening skills from this game. Additionally, they must multitask by moving toward the nearest chair while listening to music.

While attempting to reach the chair first, they can also improve their balance and speed.

While attempting to reach the chair first, they can also improve their balance and speed. Red Light/Green Light

The game Red Light, Green Light is one your kids will adore. It can be played both inside and outside.

One participant occupies the center of the room while the others are positioned on the other side. Everyone moves as quickly as possible to get to that person first when they turn around and announce, "green light."

Everyone must stop moving and freeze when that individual turns around and calls out "red light." Anyone moving after the "red light" signal is given must return to the starting line.

The winner of the game is the first person to touch the caller!

Your youngster will develop excellent physical abilities like speed, balance, and gross motor skills while playing this game. Additionally, they will work on their listening abilities.

53. Heads Up, Seven Up

The other games don't always call for a certain number of players, but this one does. You will require a minimum of 14 players. You can always modify it to suit your needs if you don't have as much. This game is perfect for a school setting.

Seven kids enter the room and move to the front. The others raised their thumbs while resting their heads on their desks. The seven kids circle their friends, touching just one thumb and pressing it downward.

They complete and then move back to the front. "Heads up, seven up," someone shouts. Those whose thumbs were touched stand up and make an educated guess about who touched them.

They get to trade places with the person if they are right. In that case, the game goes on as usual.

Your kids can engage with one another using this game. They will learn their classmates' names and grow in social competence. You can always adjust and put fewer people in the front if you have fewer than 14.

54. Who's Got the Button, Button, Button

Another calm indoor game you can play with kids is Button, Button. Everyone closes their eyes and sits in a circle with their hands out.

A person walks around the circle with a button in their hand, appearing to put it in everyone's hands. The person will hand one person the button.

Everyone opens their eyes after they're done with the circle and attempts to figure out who has the button. The group gets to walk around the circle to pass the button to someone else once they've finally guessed who it belongs to.

The kids will engage and get to know one another better thanks to this activity. Additionally, they will improve their social abilities.

55. Fantasy Play

Dress-up games, often known as fantasy play, are crucial for socialization. During this type of play, children use role-playing to make sense of their surroundings and the people in them.

They "practice" acting like adults by acting and socializing this way. They also portray the rules and traditions of their society.

Fantasy play is a fantastic social learning exercise for kids engaging with one or more companions and for younger kids playing alone.

The game involves pretending to interact with others even if the child is alone, which is a great method for them to securely act out an encounter.

Create opportunities for your youngster by setting up a dressing area in their room. To promote fresh thinking, provide several themed outfits and props and switch them up periodically.

56. Sensory Play

Children like playing together in sensory activities. There is a lot of sharing, haggling, and teamwork, whether they are playing with water, mud, or sand. It frequently inspires the imagination as well.

57. Creative Play

Children are frequently immersed in conversation while engaging in creative tasks like painting, cutting, pasting, or molding playdough.

These activities typically take place at a table where the kids are relaxed and actively playing with one another.

I have seen some of the most fascinating and intricate social interactions around an art table.

58. Reading

My all-time favorite activity has to be reading to kids because it has so many advantages. Stories are primarily about the interactions and connections between humans and animals.

Every time you read to your child, she will be exposed to the characters' social skills, problem-solving techniques, emotional expressions, and general interactions.

A young child may find it difficult to understand empathy, for instance, but you may impart the lesson through a narrative and let your child develop this quality on her own by listening.

59. Discussions

Talking with your kids in groups is a good approach to teaching them social skills in addition to reading.

Take every chance to talk to your kids about their feelings, friendships, and even the fictional characters in the stories and how they handled particular situations.

Discussing potential solutions or teaching your kids how to handle conflict with a buddy is a much more instructive experience than stepping in right away.

60. Free Play

When kids are playing freely with one another, socialization and learning happen most naturally.

You may decide to promote and offer particular activities, like an art project, but keep in mind that any time spent playing with people is spent teaching them important social skills.

Avoid letting excessive planned activities or screen time interfere with genuine play and social interaction.

61. "Give a Little Something, to Get a Little Something"

Discuss with your youngster what occurs when something doesn't go as planned. How do they feel about it?

Sometimes we have to give a little to receive a little.

Remind or prod your youngster to repeat this sentence the next time they are in a heated dispute or quarrel.

Offer suggestions and work together to find a solution. For instance, you could play with the item five minutes after your friend has, and vice versa.

62. "Teddy Bear's Picnic"

Make a picnic for the teddy bears with as many teddy visitors as your child would like and toy food!

Give your child and each bear a plate.

Is your youngster able to share the food so that everyone receives the same amount?

63. "Out and About."

Please encourage your child to interact with their friends by chatting about what they are doing, whether you are at the park or out and about with them.

Say things like, "Oh, that's what they're playing with. Can you see his construction? What is he producing, I wonder? How do you feel?"

If your youngster shows signs of interest, encourage them by showing them how to ask, "Can I play?"

If the other child receives a "no," commend them for their politeness and suggest they try again with another child. If you want, you can always play with someone else.

64. "Can I Play?"

Use the language your child could need while engaging with others whenever you play with them at home.

Sit next to your child while playing and ask, "Can I play?"

When your kid agrees, say, 'Give a little something, to get a little something.'

Discuss with your youngster what occurs when something doesn't go as planned. How do they feel about it?

Sometimes we have to give a little to receive a little.

Remind or prod your youngster to repeat this sentence the next time they are in a heated dispute or quarrel.

Offer suggestions and work together to find a solution. For instance, you could play with the item five minutes after your friend has, and vice versa.

65. "Honey Bear, Honey Bear"

Kids can become irritated when they don't get their turn, especially in games. Through this activity, students will learn that it's ok when things don't go their way; perhaps the next time will be different.

Tell your child that they will play with the honey bear. Request that they shut their eyes.

Keep wrist bells, a spoon box, a tin of pebbles, or anything else noisy hidden from your toddler. It must be loud enough for the child to hear it even when they close their eyes. This is the "honey" of the bear.

Ask your child to find the honey once you've hidden it.

Repeat the game, hiding the loud object somewhere new each time.

66. "Pitch It"

What happens when someone does something that they don't like? Discuss this with your youngster. How do they feel about it?

Together, investigate: Have your youngster "pitch" suggestions for what people can say or do to help us feel better. For instance, offering to fix anything that was broken or apologizing.

Put all your ideas in a clear bowl or jar after writing them down (on paper or popsicle sticks).

If your child ever finds themselves in a situation where something sad has occurred to them, or they have done something sad to someone else, you may look back to their suggestions and give them a plan of action.

67. "A Kindness Card."

"Kindness cards" can be made with your child. Together, you may decide on the size and shape of the cards. What "kind" pictures can you come up with to paint or draw on there together? For instance, a heart, a flower, a happy expression, playing together, and hugs...

Once completed, use these cards to reward your child for being especially kind or having a day filled with kind deeds!

Encourage them to proudly display it.

68. "Ten Stars of Kindness."

This game is excellent for teaching kids how to support people with physical disabilities. Ten stars should be drawn on the page.

Your child can fill in a star each time they act of kindness, such as holding a door open, carrying something for someone else, or asking if they need help.

Ten more stars should be added once they reach ten. Add another ten stars once they reach twenty. Continue. Will they reach 100?

Talk to your child about assisting others in various situations. Kindness is not limited to the home. Discuss the many approaches that might be beneficial to various individuals.

69. "Spread Goodwill Across the World."

Supporting and involving everyone in the community requires helping people with physical disabilities.

Have your youngster draw a cloud and a rainbow on a sheet of paper using paint or colored pencils.

Request that they stop.

Have them write out some "acts of kindness" on colored paper or paper they may color in, e.g., smile, say "hi," offer to assist with carrying groceries, etc.

Cut these "kindness acts" into the form of raindrops, and then use various lengths of string to affix them to the cloud.

Affix this somewhere for your youngster to see so they can discuss performing these deeds of compassion as frequently as possible.

70. "Being a Supportive Friend."

Learn about youth mental illness and discuss possible symptoms with your child. It can sometimes be difficult to detect when someone has a mental condition.

Can your youngster come up with encouraging phrases that they may say to a buddy who might be feeling overwhelmed?

"I'm here if you want to talk," for instance. Are there any ways I can help? Do you want me to get you an adult?

Request that your child put these in writing so they can refer to them later.

71. Playing Chess

While this game only involves two players, it can be great for teaching your child to develop analytical and social skills since they must conduct themselves maturely and patiently to sit through a full chess game. Teaching your child how to play a game like chess will be an experience and a skill they will remember for the rest of their lives. They will probably even teach their child how to play chess. Chess is a great game that has been around for centuries, and now that your child is old enough to learn, this can be a great activity for you to share that is both educational and amusing.

72. Playing Scrabble

Scrabble is another game that your child can learn and play once they have reached an age where they are old enough to understand and remember the rules, as there are many in a game like this. This game is great for children between the ages of nine and twelve, as it will help them develop their language skills and learn a deeper vocabulary. This game will also help them learn social skills, as it usually involves up to 4 players and will require both individual and teamwork.

73. Limbo

Limbo is a fun game to play with children who are rapidly growing taller and taller as the months pass, as the game will be different for them each time they play. As their height changes, the game of Limbo will change for them, which can be fun to watch as a parent. You can use anything as your pole for Limbo, from the long tree branch to a meter-long ruler stick to a piece of string! This game can be played with other family members, or your child can play this with their friends. If you play as well, your child will surely have a laugh watching you try to slide your body underneath the Limbo.

This game will teach social skills as it involves many moving parts, which means that all the people playing must work together. There will be people in charge of holding the Limbo stick, people taking their turn trying to walk under, and people watching to ensure that nobody touches the Limbo pole. These people must communicate and work together, leading to the development of stronger social skills.

74. Drawing Portraits

Drawing portraits is a fun and relaxing way for your child to spend time with you or their friends or siblings inside the house. This fun, rainy-day activity will keep your children occupied and teach them valuable social skills. Each person will have a piece of paper and a pencil. Each person will draw someone else sitting with them. If there are two people, they will draw each other. They will sit across the table and draw portraits of each other simultaneously.

When they have finished, they can then compare their portraits with one another and even exchange them. This is a great activity for teaching social skills as it challenges your child to pay close attention to another person—so close that they need to draw their face. This is a good way to show your child that paying attention to others is important and can result in something beautiful!

75. Religious Involvement

Even though not everyone will practice an organized religion, for those who feel comfortable doing so, being involved in religion presents a fantastic chance for developing social skills. The majority of religious activity is, by its very nature, communal. This gives your kids a weekly chance to socialize with other people. Your child's sense of security and belonging can grow due to their involvement in religious activities and groups.

76. Owning a Pet

You would not think that caring for and keeping an animal has anything to do with how well you get along with other people, but pets are a wonderful method to teach your kids appropriate social skills and empathy.

Children can develop trust, empathy, and care for pets while getting the love and affection they give.

Children can safely acquire compassion, empathy, and responsibility for another living being in an environment free from potential judgment by interacting with animals. Supporting your child's social skills comes with the drawback that occasionally, people are not very polite. Your child's social development can be seriously hampered if they have a bad experience with someone.

Children can develop trust, empathy, and care for pets while getting the love and affection they give.

77. Community Participation

Parents frequently consider how their child interacts with other kids when considering the development of their child's social skills. But the development of social skills extends far further than that. Educating our kids about their place in society is critical to developing their social skills.

Children frequently live and learn in a little bubble of their friends, family, and school. Children frequently lack the chance to observe how people from different backgrounds live.

Engaging your child in their community will allow them to interact with others from various backgrounds and develop an understanding of how families can vary. This idea is crucial for preventing social ills like entitlement and discrimination against those who are different.

78. Chores

Even though they aren't typically thought of as social skills-building activities, chores are a crucial component of social development. It's crucial to remember that social skills go beyond simply gaining friends and being a good friend. Social skills cover the full range of your child's societal integration.

Realizing that you must play a role in society is one of its most significant realities. You need to take care of your obligations. Chores enable the youngster to develop the skills necessary for working later in society.

79. Camps and Retreats

Children who don't get the chance to practice their social skills will frequently fall short in this regard. It's critical that parents feel at ease enabling their kids to explore the world and spend time away from home.

Retreats and camps are excellent places to practice this. Children can experience themselves outside of the family unit during camps or retreats, which is a crucial aspect of typical social development. This is further aided by the fact that many camps and retreats actively plan social skill development activities in their programs.

80. Self-introduction for Kids

A crucial life skill that gives children opportunities to feel confident, establish friends, and meet new people is the ability to introduce themselves.

In various contexts, children may be required to introduce themselves to a group, most often in their classroom or an activity group.

Make a set of opening questions and have participants respond by introducing themselves.

Make a list of questions about themselves that they must respond to (favorite food, sport, names of their friends, how old they are). They can write or draw depending on their age or level of writing proficiency.

81. "Would you rather?"

A good discussion starter with two options is "Would you rather."

Even a shy youngster may become a chatty child since this game is entertaining.

You can either go through each one (because they are all so much fun!) or pick the ones your youngster would prefer:

- Which Food Would you rather
- Superpowers: Would You Rather
- Animal Concerns
- School Would you rather
- Disney Would You Rather

82. Continue My Story

At home, we enjoy sharing stories. Every day I conjure up brand-new tales to tell my child.

Another enjoyable exercise that requires attentive listening is using stories.

One group member begins a story, pauses it at a certain point, and decides who will carry it on. The next person will continue the narrative from that point and eventually hand it off to another.

Because nobody can predict when they will take their turn, everyone must listen intently.

83. Guess What I'm Describing

Pick a subject that you can describe, like a lion or a game. Share each hint until someone correctly identifies what you are describing.

It is an animal; it is four-legged; it is wild, etc. If it is a game, what does it entail?

84. Drama Workshop

On pieces of paper, note various feelings, and place them in a bag. Each of you will pick a slip of paper and, in turn, role-play the emotion it contains.

The individual who is role-playing practices their ability to articulate their emotions.

The guessers are working on their ability to recognize emotions.

85. Keeping a Feelings Journal

For some kids, it could be challenging to articulate their emotions. Writing a feelings journal may be useful for gaining confidence while reflecting on emotions. For girls, this is a terrific one. And with prompts and a cute design, this one would make a wonderful guided notebook for teenagers.

86. Things We Have in Common

This friendship-building activity is excellent for dismantling obstacles.

Children are grouped in small groups, ideally with a variety of children who are not all close buddies. The team must identify a predetermined number of items they all have in common.

Kids get to know one another well and realize how much they may have in common with kids from various social groupings.

87. Guess Fake or Real Apology

Play a guessing game in which they must determine if an apology is sincere or not.

Give examples of various circumstances in which an apology is required. Ask the children to create a range of sincere and fictitious apologies.

Then, for laughs, go in a circle and have them recite their apologies. Each time a child apologizes, the other children must determine whether or not it was sincere and what hints they were given.

88. Compose a Letter of Apology

Your child can express their feelings and consider how their actions affect others by writing an apology letter. Use it to apologize for something they did or didn't do to their friends.

89. Help Kids Take Other People's Perspectives

The reflection on how others feel about a situation can be highly enlightening and aided by perspective-taking exercises.

Choose a range of scenarios that your children or pupils might experience:

Joe cracks a joke regarding Tim's hair. How is Tim feeling? What's Tim's mood like?

Kathy isn't included in Anna's invitation to a playdate with Emma and Lily. Why do you think Anna excluded Kathy? What was Kathy's mood when she was excluded?

90. Conflict Resolution Role-Play

Write down the typical disputes that youngsters experience on a popsicle stick. When you have about 20 students, have two of them stand in front of the class and perform the scenario depicted on the popsicle stick.

After they perform it, have the class explore various approaches to solving the issue, either as a whole or in smaller groups.

91. Model Emotions with Playdough

Playdough modeling is a fun exercise that can help kids develop their creativity, fine motor abilities, and social and emotional skills.

In this instance, we focus on the activity's social and emotional components.

Using this activity, you can start conversations about feelings and emotions and concentrate on recognizing emotions through facial expressions. Let's make a joyful face, for instance.

How can you tell this child is happy?

How do they appear?

Is the way they smile an indication, too?

92. Empathy Play / Drama Game

Play role-playing empathy games with your children. You can "professionalize" this activity to the furthest degree.

Make sure they're dressed for the occasion. Consider characters who occasionally struggle in school (the shy guy, the nerdy guy, the loner, the new kid).

Put one child in one of those roles and another in the role of the child. What does it feel like to be one of those kids? What do they want other people to do? Then, have them switch roles and role-play once more. How has your behavior changed? Do they have a greater grasp of the other person?

93. Decision-Making Games

Children can develop their social skills by playing a variety of activities that encourage decision-making. Children can learn to be persistent, cooperative, considerate, and sympathetic by playing simple sorting games.

Children must make up their minds even if their choice is incorrect at first. Children should not be punished if they make a mistake; instead, you should motivate them to try again.

94. Strength Jenga

Give each child in your group a Jenga block to start. Next, give them the task of jotting down what they see as their greatest strength or talent. As each individual adds a block to the tower, have them read their response. Finally, discuss the value of cooperation and respect for others.

95. Conversation Cubes

Thanks to this game, you can have more in-depth discussions with your children.

For children who struggle with social skills, it is also an excellent tool to use in therapy because rolling the die and answering the question significantly lessens the burden of social contact.

Six cubes, each with thought-provoking questions, are included in the set. The game covers certain fundamental social abilities, including communication abilities and listening aptitudes

96. Chill Chat Challenge

This social skills game is an excellent way to foster communication within the family and cultivate conversational skills by asking different questions to get to know everyone better.

Three categories of subjects are covered:

- Chill: simple and informal subjects (music, fashion)
- Chat: discussion of the news, social media, and personal experiences.
- Challenge: more difficult subjects, like morality or private matters

It is an excellent method to engage teenagers in conversation.

It provides a variety of themes, ranging from simple to more complex questions, and it fosters connection through sharing all types of experiences (funny anecdotes, secrets, opinions). Works well in therapy, in the classroom, and at home.

97. A Flipbook of Mistakes

These self-assurance-boosting activities will assist the teenagers in learning from their previous failures and turning them into successes.

What to do:

- Use past errors that have had the greatest impact.
- The potential causes of the failures should be recorded.
- It enhances their ability to think of the best solutions.

- Comprehending failure and its distinct causes lessens negative emotions in life.

98. Chart of Self-Appreciation

With the help of this chart, your teens will develop healthy self-esteem and learn to appreciate themselves for the right reasons.

What to do:

- Tell your teenagers to add one positive trait about themselves on the chart.
- Start modest and progressively work your way up to more significant traits.
- Thanks to this activity, your teens will learn to value and respect themselves.

99. "When You Get the Ball, Answer the Question"

Conversational balls are excellent tools for getting kids to know one another.

Conversation starters are printed on these balls. They can be played with in a variety of ways. Typically, you toss the ball while checking the question you need to answer with your thumb.

Additionally, you can pick one of the questions and pass the ball around while the children wait their turn to respond.

Interpersonal skills are encouraged via conversation balls (taking turns, eye contact, listening, responding).

100. The Dancing Chain Game

This game is a great way for little ones to develop their social skills while having fun with friends or family at the same time. This game involves some dancing or moving the body, which little boys and girls often find extremely fun. To play this game, the first person begins by doing a short dance move, or a movement such as a jump or a twirl.

The next person then has to copy the first person's movement, and then do one of their own. This chain continues, and each person must complete all of the dance moves that their friends or family members did before adding on a dance move of their own.

This game is a great way for younger children to develop their social skills because not only are they participating in a group activity, but they must also pay attention to everyone else around them and dance for others to see. The children will not even know that this game is educational because they will be having so much fun with it.

101. Three-Legged Race or Wheelbarrow Race

Having a good old-fashioned three-legged race or a wheelbarrow race are two great ways to help kids develop their social skills as well as their teamwork skills. These games are fun to play with multiple siblings, at a birthday party, or with cousins at a family get-together. It can also be played with smaller groups too!

To begin, two kids will stand two of their ankles next to each other. A parent will then tie their ankles together using a piece of ribbon or a necktie or something else similar. Then, the kids will hold onto each other and try to run as fast as they can from the starting line to the finish line, ensuring that they synchronize their steps to avoid toppling over one another. If you have many people, you can have one big race, and this will be fun for all ages.

A wheelbarrow race is quite similar except that it begins with one child lying face-down on the floor, their hands pressed to the ground on either side of their chest. The second child will lift the first child's legs off of the ground and hold onto their ankles, while the first child will hold the rest of their own body up by their arms. They will use their arms to walk along the floor or the grass and the other child will try to walk as if they are pushing a wheelbarrow all the way to the finish line!

102. Make Your Own Recycling Creations

This is a fun activity for children of all ages, and it is especially parent-friendly as it does not require much in terms of materials!

Bring your recycling bin into your craft area or the backyard with some tape, markers, stickers, and anything else your child could use to make their creation special. You can also take part in this, or your children can do it on their own. They can get creative with the recycling bin by using old boxes and containers to build anything they can imagine.

Some examples of creations that can be easily made are a robot, a city, an animal, a truck, or anything else! Encourage kids to use as many items as possible from your recycling bin. The best part about this activity is that you can put everything back into the recycling bin with no mess and no extra garbage after your child has finished.

103. Music Crafts

Doing crafts with your child is a fun way to spend an afternoon, and children of any age can do this craft. Using a toilet paper tube or a paper towel tube, take some small, dry pasta like macaroni or some small beads and fill the tube with them. Be careful that your child does not put these in their mouth as they are a choking hazard for young children. Cover each end with some paper or tissue and seal each end of it with an elastic band or some tape. Then, you are ready to decorate. Color and decorate your new musical instruments however you wish to.

Once you have finished, you are ready to "shake, shake, shake," and you will be able to make music together until your hearts are content! Babies can play music if it involves shaking, and they will enjoy hearing the sound of the shaking instruments you have made. Older children can have fun with the decoration and assembly portions of this craft, and they can even have fun trying to make sound patterns with their maracas at the end.

104. Balloon Volleyball

Outdoor volleyball can be played with any number of people, and it is just as fun with two people as it is with ten people! All you need is a volleyball and something to use as a net. Then, you can play your game by bumping and volleying the ball back and forth to each other and trying to get as many rallies as possible before the ball falls to the ground. This can be done with only two people if you want to play with your child, or they can play it with their friends.

If your child is younger, they can play this using a balloon instead of a volleyball. In this case, get on your knees and bounce the balloon, having your child try to keep it in the air using their hands and arms. Try to get a rally going for as long as possible with them. Using a balloon will be safe and fun for little ones and older ones alike, and when they get big enough, they will be able to join in on the fun with real volleyball.

105. Have a Water Fight!

Playing with water guns is every child's dream. Playing with water guns with their parents is an even bigger dream! If you offer to play with water guns with your child, it will be the happiest day of their life! Fill some water guns and run around with your child spraying them and hiding behind trees or obstacles you find along the way. You will both be laughing while also getting exercise and busting your boredom together!

106. Hopscotch

A lot of fun can be had with a piece of chalk in a driveway, and you can also help your child to develop teamwork skills as they can come up with hopscotch along with you or with their friends or siblings. Together, have the kids draw out a hopscotch shape using chalk. They can decide on the colors and the shapes together as a team.

Then, show your child how to hop through the hopscotch, landing with one foot on the single squares and two feet on the double-wide squares. Take turns trying to get through as quickly as possible or in the most creative ways you can think of. Then, try to create the most creative hopscotch shapes and arrangements possible, making it as fun and challenging as possible.

107. Doubles Jump Rope

Jumping rope is a fun way for your child to be active while having fun and for your child to learn teamwork skills with other children their age. Using a long jump rope, one child will hold on to each end, and they will need to spin the rope together in a synchronized manner to keep it spinning steadily enough for someone to jump rope in it.

Then, a third child will jump into the middle of the rope and jump each time the rope spins under their feet. The children can count together and try to jump over the rope as often as possible. This teaches them to take turns in different roles and work together for everyone to enjoy themselves.

108. Hot Potato

Hot potato is a fun game that will test your child's quick movement skills, but it also helps kids work as a team toward a common goal. This game can be played at a birthday party in a circle with a large number of kids, or it can be played with only a few kids at a time. Begin with a ball or any other small object such as a tennis ball or a pair of socks rolled up into a small bundle.

One person will begin with the ball and quickly pass it to the next person. The game aims to keep the ball from falling to the floor while passing it from one person to the next as quickly as possible. This will have all the kids working together toward a common goal, strengthening their teamwork skills in a fun and challenging way.

109. Making Dinner Together

Another way to practice etiquette and table manners is by getting your child engaged in learning about everything to do with dinner time. To do this, you can have them help you to prepare dinner from start to finish, and then they can help you serve it.

By doing this, they will be invested in the meal, and this will make them much more likely to practice their table manners as they will be feeling like a grown-up. You can remind them of some of your expectations when it comes to their table etiquette, and you can show them by demonstration.

110. Modeling for Younger Siblings

If you have multiple children, you can teach table manners by having one of the older children show the younger children what is expected. Young children look up to their siblings, and they will be very likely to copy the behavior of their older siblings. If your eldest child can model this, your younger children will want to practice it too.

111. Modeling for Your Child

Since children look up to their parents, modeling table manners for your child is one of the best ways to teach them. If your child sees you eating and generally conducting yourself in a polite way at the dinner table, they will follow your lead and do so as well. It may take some reminding, but if you continue to model this, they will better understand what is expected of them.

112. Tea Party with Stuffed Animals

Another great way to teach your child table manners is by having a fancy tea party with them and their stuffed animals. A British tea party is the epitome of etiquette and has the highest expectations for table manners, so act this out with them by having them teach their teddy bears all about table manners, and you and your child can play along with them as well.

113. Reading a Manners Book

There are many great books on the topic of table manners. If your child likes reading books with you, find a picture book at the library that talks about table manners and read this to them. They will likely be excited to try what they have learned after seeing it in the picture book.

114. Setting the Table

Having your child help you set the table will help them to learn where everything goes and how the table is set, as often children do not pay much attention to this if they show up at the table with food already in front of them. By setting the table with you, they can learn what each person needs at their place setting, where the different utensils go, what extras are needed for what kinds of food, such as condiments or seasonings, and it will give them a better overall sense of what goes into preparing for a meal at the table.

115. Clean Up the Table before Dessert

One way to teach your child about cleaning up the table and keeping things tidy is by having them clean up the table after dinner and before dessert. This will lead them to be less inclined to run away from the table immediately after they have finished eating, as they know, there is something else to look forward to after eating.

Teach them about what needs to be done, such as bringing the plates and dishes to the kitchen counter or to the sink, putting leftovers into the fridge and wiping off the table with a cloth, and then setting the table anew for dessert. This is likely to help them learn much more than trying to keep them around after dinner has finished with no incentive.

116. Going Out for Dinner

To have some fun practicing table manners with your child, make it an engaging and fun experience. Tell your child that you want to practice table manners with them by taking them out to a restaurant. Have them help you to choose the restaurant and then treat it like a fun experience and a special outing.

Your child will be excited about this occasion, and they will be excited to learn about table manners with you in this setting. Once you are there, you can have them practice ordering for themselves using please and thank you, eating with a fork or spoon, using a cloth napkin, chewing politely, and asking to be excused.

117. Bath Time Fun

This is a great way to spend some quality time with your child if they are still in their younger years. Children love baths, and spending this time with you will make it even better! Get into the bathtub with your child if they are small enough and hold onto them or sit facing them, depending on how old they are.

While you are in the bathtub with them, you can sing songs to them or teach them new words. You can also play splashing games or follow their lead as they play with their bath toys. This is a great way to develop a deeper relationship with your young child as you can bond skin-to-skin while enjoying yourselves and getting squeaky clean!

118. Photo Album Bonding Time

This one is a fun way to spend time with your child. Get out some old picture albums or old photos and sit with your child in a comfortable place. Then, show them those old family photos and see if your child recognizes the people in them!

Do they laugh at the hairstyle you had in the eighties? If you have no photo albums, you can also make one first by printing out some photos of your family and having your child help you put them into an album. They will enjoy reminiscing with you, and they will be able to see you and your other family members in new ways, well before they were born. Knowing more about your life before you had them will bond you in new ways.

119. Pre-Bedtime Reading

Before you put your child to bed, you can take some time to spend with them before they drift off to sleep. This time of day is a great time to relax with your child and share cuddles while you read them their favorite books. This can be done with children of all ages, as long as you pick books appropriate for their age levels.

This can be done for years as a wonderful bedtime routine you share. Taking some of your child's favorite books and reading them aloud will make them laugh, especially if you begin to put on funny voices and get animated as the story progresses. This part of the day will be something your child looks forward to in no time.

120. Rock Skipping

Do you ever remember going to the river or the lake with your parents and having them teach you to skip rocks? This is a great way to bond with your child now and is something that your child will remember forever. To do this, take a flat rock and gently toss it into the water, trying to make sure that it lands as flat as possible.

Then, watch as it bounces on the surface of the pond, lake, river, or pool before finally sinking to the bottom. This takes practice, and this practice is valuable time that you can share, trying to hone your skills and teaching each other new things along the way.

121. Motion Picture Marathon

Come to an agreement on which film arrangement or kind to watch. A companion of mine completed an *Avengers* long-distance race with a gathering of folks and another companion did the *Lord of the Rings* set of three with his children. It very well may be that or lighthearted comedies with your little girl.

Get some popcorn, keep awake until late, maybe even throughout the night. Make it an extraordinary occasion. You can even make it a convention. There will presumably be some startling discussions en route.

122. Climb, Camp, as well as Rock Climb

This certainly gets the experience segment. Discover a trail to climb or an outdoor place. On the off chance that you are prepared and have the best possible gear take them rock climbing. If not, locate a neighborhood rock climbing divider. There's not at all like overcoming a physical test together.

123. Go to an Amusement Park

Very little can equal the enjoyment of a major entertainment mecca. Any place you live, there is one inside driving separation. For whatever length of time that you are healthy, get out there with your youngster and have a ton of fun. The mutual adrenaline surge on a crazy ride as your stomach feels like it leaves your body will be a minute neither of you will overlook.

124. Network Administration

It's significant your teenager discovers that the world truly doesn't revolve around him/her. This doesn't need to be an intense exercise, notwithstanding. There are chances to volunteer that are compensating just as fun. Working one next to the other with your youngster that includes penance to help another will hoist your relationship.

125. Take a Road Trip

Across the nation to everything in the middle, there are experiences to be found. Ensure your youngster gets the chance to see the locales up close. Find peculiar spots to visit. The greater part of all, keep off the interstate when at all conceivable. The individuals, the nourishment, and the landscape will bring long periods of discussion.

126. Photograph Hunt

Take your high schooler on a nature climb with cameras close by, and chase the wonderful animals and scenes. Take the time heretofore to realize what creatures you may see and their conduct. This will protect you and the creatures too. Your youngster will become familiar with gratefulness for nature and the entirety of its living animals.

127. Mess Around

Host a game night at your home if your adolescents are willing. Get a bunch of snacks and play Family, Mafia (or The Werewolves of Millers Hollow, which I find superior), Catch Phrase, Over the Mountain, Four on the Couch, Three on the Couch, Two Truths and Lie, or Pictionary Down The Lane.

128. Bowling

For bowling, it's possibly the basic idea of the game and the conspicuous absence of pressure in its structure that comforts everybody. Get some snacks, snicker at the gutter-balls, and cheer for each other's strikes.

129. Show-and-Tell

This is a familiar activity to share something special! Kids will share a favorite meaningful item with others and then tune in to listen about others' favorite items. Use this as an opportunity to practice asking clarifying or meaningful questions about someone else's special something. This can be done in person or on a video chat with friends and family who live far away!

130. Top Ten

Getting to know other people, their interests, their preferences, and their stories is a big part of developing social relationships. In this activity, children will practice listening attentively to others' interests and then test their memories.

Give players a category. You can use one of these or make up your own:

- Ice cream flavors
- Fruits
- TV shows
- TV characters

Each player will think about their top ten (or five if you are playing with younger children) favorites in the category. If they would like, they can write their lists on paper.

- One player will share their top-ten list with a partner.
- The partner will then do their best to tell the rest of the group what was on the list.
- See how many players can remember! Then, switch roles and play again.

131. "Stomp, Stomp, Wink"

Body language is the name of the game in this activity. Kids will copy the leader's movements, but they'll have to be extra attentive. The leader could transfer the lead with a wink (or a blink, for players who can't wink just yet). Children will practice active listening and body-language awareness in this activity.

132. "I Tell, You Tell"

Learning about each other's lives is a foundational layer of relationships. In this activity, children will practice both sharing their own stories and listening to others' stories.

133. Back-to-Back Directed Drawing

Giving clear instructions can be harder than it sounds! In this activity, one child will give specific, clear instructions for a drawing while the other uses active listening to draw the picture. This activity will give kids a chance to work on their communication skills and hone their patience.

134. "Row Your Boat"

In this movement-based activity, you and your toddler will work together to row your boat. This simple activity will encourage your child to play cooperatively in a give-and-take manner.

- Sit cross-legged facing your child. Your child does not need to sit cross-legged and can have legs out straight if that is more comfortable.
- Hold hands in the center.
- Sing, "Row, row, row your boat gently down the stream. Merrily, merrily, merrily, merrily, life is but a dream!"
- As you sing, gently rock back and forth with one person moving forward while the other moves backward and then alternating. Working together to coordinate the rowing movement is a cooperative activity.

Repeat this several times until your child is no longer interested.

135. "You Pick, I Pick"

Sharing, cooperation, and self-control are the hallmarks of this activity. Participating in activities that others enjoy or choose is a great skill to practice for friendships and will help kids understand that they won't always get to choose the activity or game. Give kids a variety of toys to choose from, and they'll take turns picking one thing for the group to play with together.

136. City Planning

This creative adventure has kids pretending to be city planners. They'll design a city using random craft supplies you have on hand. Encourage creative thinking, problem-solving, and communication as they plan how their city will come to life!

137. Partner Yoga

Roll out your yoga mats for this cooperative activity. Partner yoga poses are a great way to build cooperative skills and communication skills as kids share how they feel in the poses and share what they need from their partners to feel supported in the poses. Plus, they're working on mindfulness and physical fitness as well.

138. "That's Me!"

This entertaining game is a hit among kids. Form a circle. One child takes the stage and introduces themselves, mentioning their favorite dish, color, or animal. The other kids with the same interests get up and exclaim, "That's me!"

139. Helping Hands

Sometimes responsibility isn't just about doing what's expected—it's about doing a little more to go the extra mile. In this activity, kids will think about ways they can be helpful to their family and how they can contribute at home outside of their regular responsibilities.

- Give kids a chance to think about some extra ways they can help around the house.
- On small rectangular pieces of paper, make "Helping Hands Coupons." On the coupons, kids can write or draw ways they can be helpful.
- Place the coupons in an envelope to save for later.
- As kids recognize a need at home or when adults could use a helping hand, coupons can be exchanged for extra help.

140. Time Tracker

Visual representations of tasks or times really help kids understand when to do tasks and help them learn the valuable skill of time management! Being able to manage time and complete tasks in a designated time interval will help kids become more responsible and will help them in the future in school.

141. Adopt a Neighbor

Encourage community and social responsibility and empathy in this helpful activity! Choose a neighbor to "adopt" and help your child do small things to brighten that neighbor's day or help them in big and small ways.

142. Predicting Characters' Feelings

Use your regular story time to build empathy skills. In this activity, you'll take time to discuss the characters' feelings and predict how they might feel about alternate events. This will help kids think about how others' actions impact feelings.

143. Mirror Storytelling

Every face tells a story. Pull out a mirror and let your child tell a highly emotional story while facing the mirror. Ask your child to notice their own facial expressions to build an understanding of how to read other people's emotions as they speak.

144. Classmate Clues

Encourage empathetic thinking all day long, even when kids are at school! In the morning, give your child the name of one classmate. Their job for the day is to notice that classmate and try to figure out how they are feeling. This will help kids grow their empathy as well as develop an understanding of others.

145. Park People Watching

Sometimes, building a little empathy can be as easy as sitting back and watching people! Head out to a park, city street, or busy area and watch the people around you. Talk with your child to encourage them to notice things about others and their experiences.

146. Empathy Map

An empathy map is a visual representation of things to consider in a situation and ways to show empathy. Kids can use this tool to predict how others are thinking and feeling and then consider what they might say and do to show empathy. Creating an empathy map helps kids really understand what empathy looks like in real life.

- At the top of the page, write a situation. This can be a made-up situation or something that your kid has actually seen. For example, you might write, "Anna brought kimchi for lunch, and people in our class told her it smelled gross."
- Draw four squares on the piece of paper, under the situation. Label them "think," "feel," "say," and "do."

In each of the sections, talk about and write what the person in the situation might think and what they might feel. Then, write what your child could say or do to show empathy in the other boxes. Let your child generate these ideas.

147. Break in the Game

Joining a game with peers is a great skill for kids to have as they get older and move toward independent, non-parent-directed play. In this activity, kids will practice joining a game that others are already playing.

148. "Mirror, Mirror"

Mirror, mirror on the wall, who has the best self-control of all? In this game, kids will mirror each other's movements as they tune in to body-language cues and exercise self-control!

149. "May I Please...?"

In this game of asking permission, kids will practice first asking and then accepting responses, even if the answer is no. Kids will take turns asking permission to move forward in the game, and the adult leader will grant or deny permission. This is great practice for exercising self-control in situations when kids might not get to do what they want to do.

150. Partner Maze

This a-maze-ing activity will give kids a big social-skills boost! Kids will work together to get through a homemade maze by using effective communication, active listening, trust, and cooperation skills.

- The adult should set up a maze using household items. You can set this up inside using chairs or

pillows or outside using outdoor toys and lawn chairs.
- Children will work together in pairs. One child will close their eyes while the other child gives verbal directions to get through the maze. Important note: Some children will not feel safe or comfortable closing their eyes. You can also choose to have the child walk backward through the maze with eyes open.
- When the first child has made it through the maze, partners will switch roles. You may choose to alter the maze slightly since the first partner has already seen the setup.

151. Grandparent Interview

Grandparents are a treasure trove of fascinating stories and interesting information! Give your child time to interview a grandparent to get to know them better. This exercise will help expand their empathy and understanding of this family member.

152. In Their Shoes

Encourage your kid to step outside of their own experiences and step into someone else's shoes for this activity. Imagining what it might be like to live a day in the life of someone else will encourage kids to think about the daily experiences of others.

CONCLUSION

Social skills are important for cohesion in the family unit, developing and maintaining friendships outside the family, participating in group events like sports or extracurricular clubs, meaningfully contributing in academic settings with peers, and engaging beyond adulthood and careers. These skills require understanding oneself and how each of us relates to others and the world around us. Meaningful connections formed through positive social skills give kids and adults a sense of belonging and connectedness that directly impacts physical and mental health and future success.

While the importance of social skills is clear, there remain a variety of paths kids can take to practice social skills. Use the activities in this book to enrich your relationships and how you help your child understand the world and others around them. Each child's path will look a little different, and that's part of what makes kids amazing! Enjoy your time growing together.

RESOURCES

Edwards. V. (2016, April 4). 9 Social Intelligence Principles Everyone Can... Science of People; Science of People. https://www.scienceofpeople.com/social-intelligence/

Morin, A. (2018, May 22). What Is Social Intelligence? Verywell Mind; Verywellmind. https://www.verywellmind.com/what-is-social-intelligence-4163839

Human Feelings Definition & Types - Biology for Kids | Mocomi. (2016, July 25). Mocomi Kids. https://mocomi.com/feelings/

Navarro, R., Yubero, S., & Larrañaga, E. (2018). A Friend Is a Treasure and May Help You to Face Bullying. Frontiers for Young Minds, 6. https://doi.org/10.3389/frym.2018.00014

Reblin, M., & Uchino, B. N. (2008). Social and emotional support and its implication for health. Current Opinion in Psychiatry, 21(2), 201–205. https://doi.org/10.1097/yco.0b013e3282f3ad89

NHS. (2021, December 21). Depression support groups. Nhs.uk. https://www.nhs.uk/mental-health/conditions/clinical-depression/support-groups/

Cohut, M. (2018, February 23). Socialization: How does it benefit mental and physical health? Www.medicalnewstoday.com. https://www.medicalnewstoday.com/articles/321019

Monroe, J. (2018, July 2). The Importance of Teen... Newport Academy; Newport Academy. https://www.newportacademy.com/resources/empowering-teens/teen-friendships/

Pescaru, M. (2018, April 10). The Importance Of The Socialization Process For The Integration Of The Child In The Society. Articles R.U.S., XIV(2), 18–26. https://ideas.repec.org/a/aar/jurnal/vny2018i2a2.html

Wahjudi, J. W., Findyartini, A., & Kaligis, F. (2019, July 12). The relationship between empathy and stress: a cross-sectional study among undergraduate medical students. Korean Journal of Medical Education, 31(3), 215–226. https://doi.org/10.3946/kjme.2019.132

Soulsby, L. K., & Bennett, K. M. (2015). Marriage and Psychological Wellbeing: The Role of Social Support.

Psychology, 06(11), 1349–1359. https://doi.org/10.4236/psych.2015.611132

Brody, J. E. (2017, June 12). Social Interaction Is Critical for Mental and Physical Health. The New York Times. https://www.nytimes.com/2017/06/12/well/live/having-friends-is-good-for-you.html

Hillside. (2020, July 8). Why Your Child Is Acting Out & Appropriate Ways To Respond. Hillside. https://hside.org/reasons-children-act-out/

Seabrook, E. M., Kern, M. L., & Rickard, N. S. (2016). Social Networking Sites, Depression, and Anxiety: A Systematic Review. JMIR Mental Health, 3(4), e50. https://doi.org/10.2196/mental.5842

Greenberg, B. (2018, June 18). 5 Ways to Help Teens Set Boundaries With Friends. US News & World Report; U.S. News & World Report. https://health.usnews.com/wellness/for-parents/articles/2018-02-13/5-ways-to-help-teens-set-boundaries-with-friends

Mcilroy, A. T. (2021, September 9). 30 Simple Role Play Ideas for Kids. Empowered Parents. https://empoweredparents.co/role-play-ideas-for-kids/

LisaLisa. (2020, January 15). 7 Activities to Help Kids Learn Key Social Skills. https://nighthelper.com/7-activities-to-help-kids-learn-key-social-skills/

Waterstone on Augusta. (2018, August 14). Importance of Socialization for Alzheimer's and Dementia Care - Waterstone. Waterstone on Augusta. https://www.waterstoneonaugusta.com/importance-of-socialization-for-alzheimers-and-dementia-care/

Made in United States
North Haven, CT
20 November 2022